Western Steam in Devon and Cornwall

MICHAEL WELCH

Capital Transport

ISBN 978-1-85414-327-3

Published by
Capital Transport Publishing
P.O. Box 250, Harrow, HA3 5ZH

Printed by
CS Graphics
Singapore

© Michael Welch 2009

Front cover: The St Ives branch is steeply graded, down trains facing a continuous 1 in 60 climb all of the way from Lelant to the top of the incline just before Carbis Bay station is reached. A similar gradient applies in the reverse direction but at least there is a brief section of level track at the approach to Carbis Bay. In this picture 4500 Class 2-6-2T No.4564 appears to be making heavy weather of the climb towards Carbis Bay hauling a relatively heavy five-coach train on 12th August 1961. Passengers were no doubt enjoying the breathtaking views of St Ives Bay from the carriage windows. *Roy Patterson*

Back Cover: Glorious Devon personified. The infant river Culm trickles by on the right and puffy clouds scud across the sky as 1400 Class 0-4-2T No.1451 sits in Hemyock station with a train to Tiverton Junction. One wonders if any passengers deigned to appear. If so, they would have to be patient because the Hemyock branch trains were reputedly the slowest passenger workings in Great Britain and the 7½ mile trip could take up to 58 minutes. In the background is the dairy which for many years provided so much of the line's traffic. *R. C. Riley*

Title page: The 34¾ mile-long Plymouth to Launceston line is one of the most attractive routes included in this album. The route followed a number of lush river valleys but other sections skirted the wild and desolate fringes of Dartmoor – the contrast could not be more marked. This shot shows an unidentified Plymouth to Tavistock train crossing a slender, lofty viaduct, just south of Tavistock, that takes the line across the river Walkham which is out of sight among the tangle of branches at the bottom of the picture. *John Beckett*

Introduction

Golden sands with an almost Mediterranean blue sea stretching into the distance, a superb coastline dotted with sandy coves and ancient fishing villages steeped in history, and an agreeably mild climate. Is it any wonder that Devon and Cornwall are two of the best-loved counties in England that have attracted many generations of holiday-makers?

The expansion of the railway network played a crucial role in developing the south-west of England, and the Bristol & Exeter Railway (B&ER) opened from London to Exeter (via Bristol) on 1st May 1844. The South Devon Railway was responsible for the next section westwards as far as Plymouth and this opened throughout in April 1849. This included one of the most beautiful stretches (arguably *the* most beautiful) on any railway line in Great Britain, the section along the river Exe estuary with its distant views towards Exmouth, the journey along the sea wall between Dawlish Warren and Teignmouth and then a further stretch alongside the river Teign before Newton Abbot is reached. It was originally Brunel's intention to work the Exeter to Plymouth line atmospherically, parts of the line being engineered with very steep gradients that have plagued operations ever since. The West Cornwall Railway opened from Truro to Penzance in 1852, leaving a gap between Plymouth and Truro that was eventually bridged by the Cornwall Railway in 1859. It should be noted that the West Cornwall Railway was built to the standard gauge whereas the other lines mentioned were constructed to the broad gauge.

Most of the branch lines in the area covered by this album were promoted by local people who merely wished to see the town in which they lived connected to the rail network, thus enabling passengers and goods to be transported much more speedily than had previously been possible in an age when the horse and cart still predominated. In many cases they struggled to raise the necessary capital and had to be rescued by larger concerns, with the result that the original local company which had pioneered a particular line soon lost its identity and faded into history. Some of the Cornish branches began life as mineral lines and their origins can be traced back to the very earliest days of railways. Trains conveying sea-sand, china clay and granite started running between Bodmin and Wadebridge as early as 1834 and were the first steam-hauled trains in Cornwall. In complete contrast the route from Newquay to Chacewater was a very late arrival on the scene, being completed by the Great Western Railway (GWR) in 1905. This line was closed in February 1963 and reportedly some passengers on the final train had also travelled on the first train over the route – quite an achievement! Perhaps the most interesting branch line was that from Yelverton, on the Plymouth to Launceston line, to Princetown, on the slopes of Dartmoor, which climbed to a height of 1,350ft above sea level and probably offered the best vistas of any route included in this book.

During the early years of the twentieth century the GWR invested considerable resources in the development of its trunk routes, one of the most noteworthy schemes being the opening of the Reading–Taunton line, dubbed the 'new direct route to the west'. This reduced journey times between Paddington and the west of England, which greatly improved access to the west country from the capital. The GWR also assiduously promoted tourist traffic, this being done through a series of publications extolling the benefits of a visit to a particular holiday resort or area, and often this publicity material was produced on a joint basis between railway and resort. The first of these books was published in 1904 and, predictably perhaps, it focused on the Cornish Riviera which was described as an ideal winter health and pleasure resort; a volume about Devon, titled 'The Shore of the Sea Kings', was published two years later. This identified the county, a trifle unrealistically perhaps, as 'one of the great holiday haunts of the Empire'. In addition to a prolific output of books and guides, the GWR also publicised its alluring holiday locations with more than one hundred sets of lantern slides, accompanied by relevant printed lecture notes, which were available for showing to clubs, schools and similar organisations. There was even a range of jigsaw puzzles to promote the GWR's services, encourage people to travel and generally strengthen the company's brand image as the best route to leisure, history and heritage. The inter-war years brought new challenges, not least the steady drift of passengers and goods away from rural branch lines as a result of competition from road transport. The GWR responded by opening a number of new halts built to make rail transport more convenient for rural communities and these often had a characteristic 'pagoda' type waiting shelter with a short wooden-edged platform. It also expanded its own network of bus routes which connected with rail-heads and complemented its own routes. Another innovation during this period was the introduction of camping coaches at especially picturesque locations, the most noteworthy, perhaps, being Dawlish Warren, Gara Bridge and Marazion.

The end of the Second World War heralded the elimination of many branch and secondary routes, most of which served sparsely populated areas and, indeed, it is debatable whether these lines had ever made a profit at any time during their existence. The scenic byways to Moretonhampstead and Princetown were shut in the 1950s while many more followed during the following decade, forced out of business by the huge rise in private motoring. On the main lines, however, the picture was not quite as bleak, as the advent of paid holidays after the war led to a huge upsurge in week-end holiday traffic, which continued throughout the 1950s until the late Doctor (later Lord) Beeching decided that the retention of a massive fleet of rolling stock purely to cater for this seasonal flow was uneconomic, and holiday trains were quickly phased out. Examination of the summer 1961 public timetable reveals a fair number of services which left places such as Manchester, Bradford and Nottingham late on a Friday night with arrival times at Paignton, for example, around 7am on the Saturday morning which was hardly the best way to start a holiday. In addition to the scheduled trains many unadvertised reliefs also operated and the density of traffic can be gauged from the observations at Newton Abbot on the night of Friday 28th/Saturday 29th July 1961, when no fewer than 38 westbound loaded passenger trains were recorded by a local enthusiast. Could this period, almost at the end of the romantic steam age, have been the heyday of steam in Devon and Cornwall?

Compilation of this album has been a wonderfully rewarding task and I would like to express my sincere appreciation to all those photographers who had the foresight to record everyday scenes for posterity in the first place, and for their willingness to make their irreplaceable transparencies available for publication, thus reaching a much wider audience. Slides from the collection of the late R.C. Riley have been kindly provided by Rodney Lissenden. In addition, Chris Evans, David Fakes, John Langford and Graham Mallinson have scrutinized the manuscript and suggested many corrections and worthwhile improvements to the text. Design and typesetting by Lucy Day. I accept responsibility for any errors that have remained undetected.

M.S.W.
Burgess Hill,
West Sussex,
January 2009

Contents

The 44¾ miles-long line from Taunton to Barnstaple was originally promoted by the Devon & Somerset Railway who were authorised by Parliament in 1864 to build a broad-gauge route from Barnstaple to a junction with the Bristol & Exeter Railway (B&ER) just outside Taunton. Work commenced from the east in 1865 but very slow progress was made and by the summer of 1871 only the first 7¼ miles from (what is now known as) Norton Fitzwarren to Wiveliscombe had been completed. This small section opened for traffic on 8th June of that year, but after that reasonable progress ensued and the rest of the line was brought into use on 1st November 1873. The line was converted to standard gauge in 1881. A connection between the GWR (which had absorbed the B&ER in 1877) and the LSWR was laid at Barnstaple and came into use in 1887. This did not permit direct running from Taunton into Barnstaple LSWR station, however, and that was not possible until a new curve was installed in 1905. In June 1960 the GWR Barnstaple Victoria Road station was closed and henceforth trains from Taunton used the SR Barnstaple Junction station. Two sections of the route were in Somerset and therefore outside the scope of this album, but Morebath Junction, where the Exe Valley Line from Exeter converged, was definitely in Devon! Here, an unknown 4300 Class 2-6-0 passes over the junction with a Taunton to Barnstaple train on 8th June 1961. *John Beckett*

The Taunton to Barnstaple line skirted the southern slopes of Exmoor and apart from Dulverton, which is located in Somerset, and South Molton, it served very few intermediate settlements of any size. Alas, both of these stations were located some way from the places they purported to serve. At least the small village of Morebath, just visible in the distance in this shot, was close to the railway but is hardly likely to have produced much custom for the nearby Morebath Junction Halt. An unidentified 4300 Class 'Mogul' approaches the halt with a Barnstaple to Taunton working on a rather overcast 8th June 1961. Fortunately for the photographer the train's appearance coincided with a gap in the clouds, which has been known to happen very occasionally! *John Beckett*

The train seen in the previous picture rounds a curve and threads a very deep cutting at the approach to Morebath Junction Halt. The countryside in this sparsely populated area of north Devon is really outstanding, but the lack of potential passengers proved to be the line's undoing and the inevitable closure came on 3rd October 1966. This route offered the most direct way of reaching the popular north Devon holiday resort of Ilfracombe and on Saturdays in the summer it really came into its own with a number of holiday trains from London, the Midlands and north of England. Most of these deigned to stop at the more important intermediate stations. After the comparatively feverish activity on summer Saturdays, the line always 'rested' on Sundays. *John Beckett*

South Molton station, looking towards Taunton, on 3rd May 1964. This station was roughly a half-way point between Dulverton and Barnstaple Junction, and was equipped with water cranes and their attendant braziers, which were known colloquially as 'fire devils'. The principal station building and signal box were located on the down side, the main building being tile-hung no doubt to deter the worst of the south-westerly gales that rage in these parts. Being one of the more important intermediate stations on the route, BR had seen fit to install electric lighting at some stage in contrast to neighbouring stations which retained gas lighting but other station 'furniture' had remained untouched for generations. In 1963, for example, B&ER chairs still graced the waiting room here while the despatch of luggage was evidently not one of South Molton station's strong points because B&ER luggage labels were reportedly still in the racks almost ninety years after the line opened! *Roy Patterson*

The line between Braunton and Ilfracombe was one of the most steeply graded in the country, Mortehoe & Woolacombe station, which was a summit in both directions, being situated at 600ft above sea level. Trains from Braunton faced a fearsome, almost six miles-long climb, largely at 1 in 40/41, from the platform end while those starting from Ilfracombe had to contend with a continuous 1 in 36 gradient for 3¾ miles as far as Mortehoe and this from a standing start. There were magnificent views of the Bristol Channel as trains gained height just outside Ilfracombe station, but passengers aboard incoming workings were probably more concerned that the braking system was fully operational as their train approached Ilfracombe station down the very steep incline which was probably a rather frightening experience for some. Here 4300 Class 'Mogul' No.6326 ascends the 1 in 40 near Mortehoe with (what appears to be) an inter-regional holiday train in August 1964. A train of this length would almost certainly have been banked, but on this occasion the assisting engine is hidden by the exhaust being emitted by No.6326. *Alan Reeve*

The line between Braunton and Ilfracombe was one of the most steeply graded in the country, Mortehoe & Woolacombe station, which was a summit in both directions, being situated at 600ft above sea level. Trains from Braunton faced a fearsome, almost six miles-long climb, largely at 1 in 40/41, from the platform end while those starting from Ilfracombe had to contend with a continuous 1 in 36 gradient for $3\frac{1}{4}$ miles as far as Mortehoe and this from a standing start. There were magnificent views of the Bristol Channel as trains gained height just outside Ilfracombe station, but passengers aboard incoming workings were probably more concerned that the braking system was fully operational as their train approached Ilfracombe station down the very steep incline which was probably a rather frightening experience for some. Here 4300 Class 'Mogul' No.6326 ascends the 1 in 40 near Mortehoe with (what appears to be) an inter-regional holiday train in August 1964. A train of this length would almost certainly have been banked, but on this occasion the assisting engine is hidden by the exhaust being emitted by No.6326. *Alan Reeve*

The 4¼ miles-long branch from Seaton Junction, on the Waterloo to Exeter main line, to Seaton was authorised on 13th July 1863 and opened for traffic on 16th March 1868. It passed through the villages of Colyton and Colyford, terminating at a station on the west bank of the river Axe at a spot convenient for the town centre. The branch led a quiet existence and rarely had a high profile, with LSWR M7 Class 0-4-4Ts being the most common motive power for many years. In 1963, however, the line was taken over by the WR who lost no time in introducing former GWR 6400 Class 0-6-0PTs to the branch and in this photograph No.6430 presents a somewhat incongruous sight at Colyton hauling a northbound train on 12th July 1963. Services were later dieselised but in early 1965 a shortage of diesel units occurred and 1400 class 0-4-2Ts were drafted onto the branch for a brief period. The line was quite busy during the short summer holiday season, but passengers were decidedly thin on the ground during the winter period and this proved to be the line's undoing, the branch closing completely from 7th March 1966. In 1970 the Seaton & District Tramway was opened as a tourist attraction between Seaton and Colyford using redundant equipment from Eastbourne. In 1980 the 2ft 9in gauge line was extended to Colyton so, once again, it is possible to reach this location by rail! *R. C. Riley*

SEATON BRANCH

In early 1965 there was a short-lived motive power crisis in the Exeter district when a large number of diesel multiple units were out of service simultaneously and there were insufficient units available to cover the advertised train service. The WR had to resort to desperate measures to meet their commitments and in a scene more reminiscent of the Exe Valley or Chalford, 1400 Class 0-4-2T No.1450 is seen near Colyford with a Seaton Junction to Seaton train on 13th February 1965. Steam enthusiasts probably greeted the news of steam's comeback with glee, but what a pity all of the M7 Class 0-4-4Ts had gone by that time. *Roy Patterson*

Coaching stock experts will immediately identify the location of this photograph from the Barry Railway vehicle in the background which latterly was used exclusively on the Tiverton Junction to Hemyock branch line. It is, of course, Tiverton Junction and the picture shows an auto train bound for Tiverton being propelled by 1400 Class 0-4-2T No.1451 on a sunny 15th June 1962. The B&ER's main line from Taunton to Exeter, the tracks of which are behind the signal box, was opened in various stages and completed on 1st May 1844. The route was engineered by Brunel and had moderate gradients, apart from the fairly steep climbs up to Whiteball tunnel, with Tiverton Junction station being on the long, gentle descent towards Exeter. Virtually everything of railway interest seen in this picture has since been swept away and a new station, Tiverton Parkway, was built at a new location and now caters for passenger traffic from a wide catchment area. *R. C. Riley*

TIVERTON JUNCTION STATION

The decline of BR steam traction in the mid-1960s was a painful experience for steam enthusiasts as many of the remaining locomotives were poorly maintained and in a deplorable external condition. So, photographers who wanted a picture of a reasonably polished engine sometimes had to clean it themselves, even if it meant getting their hands dirty! In this picture three enthusiasts are seen cleaning 1400 Class 0-4-2T No.1450 at Tiverton Junction on 23rd August 1964 prior to its journey along the Hemyock branch. The branch was regularly diesel-worked by this time but the enthusiasts involved just happened to be friends of the Tiverton Junction stationmaster, Fred Pugh, who had arranged for No.1450 to be diagrammed especially for his friends' enjoyment. As the old saying goes, 'it's not what you know, but who you know'. Here, the three friends are seen putting in some elbow grease in an effort to restore No.1450 to a respectable condition. They are (left to right) the late John Phillips, the late Chris Gammell and John Smallwood. Let us hope their efforts were rewarded with some worthwhile pictures. This may have been steam traction's final appearance on the branch – who knows? *John Langford*

Dignity restored! A portrait of No.1450 shunting at Tiverton Junction prior to taking its train along the Hemyock branch on 23rd August 1964. Unfortunately, the unofficial cleaners did not have time to 'have a go' at the top of the boiler, for which ladders would normally have been needed, but even so the engine looks quite presentable. By this date only half a dozen of these locomotives survived, mostly based at Gloucester for working the Chalford auto trains, but No.1450 was one of two examples (the other was No.1442) shedded at Yeovil. In early 1965 there was a temporary shortage of diesel units for working the South Devon branches to Lyme Regis and Seaton and both machines were transferred to Exmouth Junction shed for duty on the Seaton branch. They did not last long on this unaccustomed work and were withdrawn simultaneously in May 1965, being officially the last of their class. Both of the aforementioned examples subsequently survived into preservation. *John Langford*

The 7½ miles-long Hemyock branch, originally known as the Culm Valley Light Railway, was authorised under an Act of Parliament on 15th May 1873 and the standard gauge line was opened on 29th May 1876. The line followed the tortuous course of the river Culm but opposition from local landowners forced the line around even tighter curves than those originally planned. There was an overall 15mph speed limit and it was the fireman's job to open and close level crossing gates. All of this did little to facilitate speedy travel along the route which reputedly offered the slowest journey times of any passenger train on the BR system, some trains taking almost an hour for the journey. The first station after Tiverton Junction (apart from a halt) was Uffculme where 1400 Class 0-4-2T No. 1471, hauling the 8.45am from Tiverton Junction, was photographed in the clear morning sunshine on 29th September 1962. *Roy Patterson*

The train in the previous picture is seen again, this time at Culmstock, which was the next station along the line from Tiverton Junction. Rather unusually, road vehicles had to cross the running line to reach the goods yard. The station here was unstaffed from 2nd May 1960 so strictly speaking it became a halt, but neither railway publications nor the station running-in boards were changed. For a time a lunchtime train from Tiverton Junction to Uffculme was extended to Culmstock on Saturdays, so the run-round loop there at least saw a modicum of use.
Roy Patterson

The Hemyock branch had an indefinable charm and character all of its own as exemplified here in this delightful shot of 1400 Class No.1450 crossing a lane at Whitehall, a tiny hamlet between Culmstock and Hemyock. A small halt, located on the right of the picture beyond the crossing, was opened here on 27th February 1933. There was also a short siding operated by a ground frame. This photograph was taken on 23rd August 1964. *John Langford*

Photographed on the same day as the previous picture when the engine had been specially rostered and cleaned by enthusiasts, No.1450 is depicted at Hemyock with a loaded milk train destined for Tiverton Junction. Oh dear, somebody overlooked cleaning the back of the bunker! In BR days at least the passenger train service along the line appears to have been unbalanced with four down trains and five up workings advertised in the winter 1953 timetable. In addition there was the late morning short working to Uffculme already mentioned. *Roy Patterson*

The classic view of a 1400 Class 0-4-2T locomotive and its short train awaiting departure from Hemyock with the placid waters of the river Culm in the foreground. The locomotive is No.1471 and the train is the 10.30am to Tiverton Junction: this picture was taken on 29th September 1962. The rather dilapidated coach is an ancient Barry Railway five-compartment gas-lit specimen, one of two identical vehicles that were commandeered for use on the line in 1950. Both were withdrawn shortly after this shot was taken and replaced by two Thompson-designed four-compartment LNER carriages. These were electrically lit but the very slow speeds on the branch were insufficient to operate their dynamos so they had to be hooked up to a battery charger at night. They normally worked singly but on 7th September 1963, the final day of passenger services, they ran together with No.1421 providing the motive power. Apart from a fair-sized crowd that gathered at Hemyock to witness the departure of the last train, few local people took any interest in the proceedings because they had doubtless long since deserted the railway for other, quicker forms of transport. Milk trains continued to operate until 3rd November 1975, after which date this tranquil backwater faded into history. *Roy Patterson*

Supervised by three dairy personnel and one BR employee, a milk tank moves across the road under its own momentum at Hemyock, also on 23rd August 1964. Wagons were presumably fly-shunted or moved by gravity but in the event of any problems the milk factory had a winch that could be used to pull wagons over the road while a flagman halted traffic. This seems at first sight to be a wonderfully archaic way of operating but at least it achieved the desired result. In order to collect loaded wagons a locomotive would propel a train of milk tanks across the road but locomotives were not, apparently, permitted to cross the road nor enter the dairy premises. One wonders how many Londoners realised that their daily 'pinta' started its journey in such a fashion. *John Langford*

HEMYOCK BRANCH

A train from Tiverton rests at Tiverton Junction station on 3rd June 1963: motive power is 1400 Class 0-4-2T No.1471. Tiverton Junction engine shed, which was latterly a sub shed of Exeter, can be seen in the background. The first shed at this location is thought to have been erected in 1848 when the Tiverton branch opened, but later the shed also housed engines working the Hemyock branch. Tiverton Junction station was remodelled in 1932 and the original shed was swept away and replaced by the building seen here. *Rodney Lissenden*

A lady with a child in a push chair, station staff engaged in conversation and a member of the train crew looking out from his cab; this was the scene at Tiverton station on 22nd August 1959 as an auto train for Tiverton Junction awaits departure. Note also the buses standing outside the adjacent garage, vehicles that would be museum pieces today. The 4½ miles-long broad gauge line from Tiverton to Tiverton Junction was the first branch to be opened in Devon and dated from 12th June 1848; the line was built as a double track route but in the event only one line was laid. The route's principal point of interest was a splendid aqueduct which carried the Grand Western canal across the tracks, this being built with separate arches for the proposed 'up' and 'down' running lines. The canal was neglected for many years but was restored some years ago, ironically, however, the course of the railway has largely reverted to nature. Latterly, there were around a dozen trips along the branch each weekday, the service being almost entirely self-contained with little through running to other destinations. The line was converted to standard gauge on 29th June 1884. Passenger services just outlived those on the neighbouring Exe Valley line, being withdrawn on 5th October 1964, while freight traffic survived until 5th June 1967. *Alan Jarvis*

TIVERTON JUNCTION TO TIVERTON

A Penzance to Manchester train approaches Cowley Bridge Junction, where the former SR route to Okehampton diverged from the WR main line, behind 'Castle' Class 4-6-0 No.5029 *Nunney Castle* on 22nd August 1963. This may have been a 'dated' summer Saturday holiday train because by this time WR main line steam traction in this area was very much in decline, as exemplified here by No.5029's dirty condition and the presence of a 'Hymek' diesel locomotive just visible in the shot on the extreme right. Built in 1934, *Nunney Castle* remained in service until December 1963 and was fortunate enough to survive into preservation. *Colour-Rail*

A train of Blue Circle cement wagons makes a colourful sight as it heads southwards past Cowley Bridge Junction, also on 22nd August 1963, with 2884 Class 2-8-0 No.2891 in command. The 2884 Class was a later version of the 2800 Class locomotives that were the first 2-8-0 goods engine design to run in Great Britain. The 2884s had outside steam pipes, large side-window cabs and were slightly heavier. This is a block train of the type that BR were heavily promoting at that time as the traditional mixed goods trains, which were deemed to be uneconomic, were quickly being phased out. *Colour-Rail*

An unidentified westbound train leaves Exeter St David's behind smartly turned out 'Castle' Class 4-6-0 No.5065 *Newport Castle* in September 1960. The vehicle immediately behind the engine is a Gresley-designed brake carriage whilst the next coach is a BR Standard kitchen car, one of a quite rare breed, compared to other BR Standard coaching stock fleets, as a total of only 41 was constructed. A mere ten vehicles were in service at the time of this picture, a further 31 being built in 1962/3. The section of line from Exeter to Newton Abbot was commissioned in stages and used the atmospheric principle which was in vogue for a short time. The line opened throughout in February 1848. *Colour-Rail*

The Exe Valley line was built in two parts. The Exe Valley Railway Company obtained an Act on 30th June 1874 for the construction of a line from Stoke Canon, just north of Exeter, to Tiverton. The Tiverton & North Devon Railway was authorised in 1875 to build a line northwards from Tiverton to connect with the Devon & Somerset Railway's Taunton to Barnstaple route at Morebath Junction. In the event the latter section of line was the first to carry traffic, the opening date being 1st August 1884. The southern section opened on 1st May 1885. Both lines were built to the standard gauge and soon came under the control of the GWR. A variety of classes appeared on branch trains, including 4500 2-6-2Ts and pannier tank engines, but the 1400 Class 0-4-2Ts, working auto trains, were probably most associated with the route. In this shot, taken on 15th June 1963, 1400 Class 0-4-2T No.1451 is depicted waiting to leave Platform 2 at Exeter St David's station with the 12.45pm to Dulverton. *Gerald Daniels*

Photographed on a rather gloomy day, 16th April 1963, 1400 Class 0-4-2T No.1442 leaves Thorverton hauling a rather strange formation comprising one passenger-carrying coach and two vans. Part of the station is just visible in the background and the station building, signal box and goods shed, plus numerous signals, can just be discerned. The private siding, which dated from 1898, on the left of the picture served a mill, imported grain being shipped into Avonmouth docks and brought to Thorverton for milling. This traffic continued for some years after the passenger service had been withdrawn, the last train running on 30th November 1966. *John Beckett*

There are no prizes for guessing the name of the meandering river seen in this illustration. A trip along the Exe Valley line offered one of the most enjoyable journeys one could wish for as exemplified here by this picture of the 2.08pm Exeter St David's to Tiverton train near Thorverton on 11th September 1962. What a pity the sun was not shining to add a bit of sparkle to the shot! Motive power is a nicely cleaned 1400 Class 0-4-2T, No.1451, hauling *Thrush*, one of two named auto trailers. *John Beckett*

A train from Exeter St David's drifts into Cadeleigh behind rather unkempt 1400 Class engine No.1451 on 3rd July 1963. Sadly, there are no passengers visible in the leading coach, this tending to justify BR's decision to close the line. The closure was authorised by the government and implemented on 7th October 1963; it should be noted, however, that Tiverton station continued to be served by trains to and from Tiverton Junction until 5th October 1964. The running-in board was double-sided, apparently to catch the attention of motorists on the nearby main road. The signalman can be seen walking along the platform before exchanging the single line tokens with the fireman. *R. C. Riley*

Like so many rural stations constructed back in the days when railway companies spared no expense, stone-built Cadeleigh was decorated with ornate chimney pots and delicately carved barge boards. The premises here were known as 'Cadeleigh & Bickleigh' until 1st May 1906 when the name was abbreviated to simply Cadeleigh, to avoid confusion with Bickleigh station on the Plymouth to Launceston line. The goods shed, on the left, was served by a loop line that went around the back of the platform. There was no footbridge at Cadeleigh, passengers being obliged to use the foot crossing. Following closure the station area became a highways depot for the local council, but in 1997 the site was purchased privately and the station buildings renovated prior to reopening as the Devon Railway Centre. *Gerald Daniels*

Not all Exe Valley trains were powered by 1400 Class engines and, as previously mentioned, other classes sometimes deigned to appear. In this portrait, taken at Tiverton station on 22nd August 1959, an unidentified pannier tank locomotive waits to leave in charge of a train to Exeter. The locomotive's fireman appears to be turning off the water crane valve as two other members of staff look on. Tiverton station was built of stone and boasted some particularly attractive features, especially the elegant footbridge which had very wide staircases to both platforms. Tiverton was for many years the third largest town in Devon and during its heyday the station, which was also served by trains to Tiverton Junction station on the main line to Paddington, had a complement of more than thirty staff. *Alan Jarvis*

The 3.28pm Bampton to Exeter train, propelled by 1400 Class 0-4-2T No.1450, leaves Cove Halt on 15th June 1963. This halt dated from 9th June 1924 and was equipped with a classic GWR pagoda waiting shelter, the only one on the Exe Valley line. A thirteen-lever signal box was originally provided here but this was downgraded to a ground frame in 1923. *Gerald Daniels*

Sheep grazing contentedly in the field, puffy clouds scudding across the sky and glorious Devon countryside. What more could one wish for? Railway enthusiasts would immediately say 'a clean 1400 Class locomotive on an auto train to enhance the scene'. The location is near the tiny hamlet of Holmingham (there was never a station at that location) where the river Batherm, which rises on the Brendon Hills, flows into the river Exe. The 3.30pm Bampton to Exeter train passes over the attractive girder bridge across the Exe on 8th June 1961. The identity of the locomotive is unknown, but does it really matter? *John Beckett*

Bampton station was one of the prettiest and best maintained on the Exe Valley line and is seen here in this illustration which shows an auto train to Exeter entering the station on 14th September 1963. The station was surrounded by mature trees on all sides which added to its delightful rural atmosphere. The main station building is almost totally concealed by the large bush but the waiting shelter on the opposite platform is clearly visible. The service along the line comprised six trains each way until 1928 from which time eight trains were advertised in each direction between Exeter and Dulverton, with four additional services to and from Tiverton. By 1961 this total had been reduced slightly with ten through trains plus a couple of short workings to Tiverton. *Alan Jarvis*

A lady ambles along the platform at Bampton pushing a baby in a pram as 1400 Class 0-4-2T No.1471 prepares to leave with an unidentified Dulverton-bound working on 3rd July 1963. The stone-built principal station building is visible in this picture together with the goods yard in the background. The yard had a cattle pen, loading dock and crane but in some ways the most interesting feature was a siding into a quarry that went off on the extreme left. The limestone quarry dated from around 1898 and ceased production in 1950. The twenty-two lever signal box was located opposite the goods shed and only a small part of its roof can be seen. *R. C. Riley*

A down goods train, hauled by 2884 Class 2-8-0 No.3848, trundles past City Basin Junction, Exeter, on 5th July 1961. This was the point at which the Teign Valley branch line to Heathfield diverged from the main Exeter to Plymouth route, the junction being clearly visible in the shot. The 2884 Class was the Collett version of the Churchward 2800 Class, a design that really stood the all-important test of time, being the GWR's standard goods engine throughout the company's existence. The prototype appeared in 1903 and the last of the Churchward locomotives was constructed in 1919. Almost twenty years later the first of the locomotives built under Collett entered service, these locomotives having detail differences as previously mentioned. No.3848 was among the last to be built, in May 1942, and was withdrawn in July 1965. *R. C. Riley*

EXETER TO NEWTON ABBOT

Exeter St Thomas station is depicted in this illustration which dates from 4th March 1961. At that time the premises still retained an attractive train shed but this was swept away later in the 1960s to leave bare and windswept platforms that were hardly an inducement to 'go by train'. The station was opened on 30th May 1846 by the South Devon Railway and for a short time was served by atmospheric trains. Improvements undertaken during the following year included construction of the train shed, larger offices and lengthening of the platforms to 260ft. The main building survives in commercial use. Latterly the station may not have been particularly inviting to prospective passengers but at least it had the compensation of being much more convenient to the city centre than St David's station. *Roy Denison*

Holiday-makers relax in the sunshine as 'Hall' Class 4-6-0 No.5950 *Wardley Hall* approaches Dawlish with an unidentified eastbound train on a sunny 31st July 1961. Judging by the coaching stock it is likely that this working was bound for somewhere on the Eastern Region. The car park on the right of the shot is full of vehicles that today would be considered museum pieces, similarly the corporation dust cart which has just crept into the picture on the extreme right. *Colour-Rail*

The magnificent stretch of railway between Exeter and Teignmouth is one of the best known and most easily recognisable in Great Britain and seems to be almost everybody's favourite section of former Western Region line. The weather conditions were not at their best when this shot was taken but despite the haze a stirring image has resulted. The train is the up 'Torbay Express', hauled by immaculate 'Castle' Class 4-6-0 No.5059 *Earl St Aldwyn,* and this picture was taken between Dawlish and Dawlish Warren on 3rd July 1957. The viewpoint is Langstone Rock which provides a splendid panoramic vista of trains approaching from both directions. *R. C. Riley*

EXETER TO NEWTON ABBOT

The 'Torbay Express' is seen again on the South Devon coast. Happy holiday-makers laze on the beach as 'Castle' Class 4-6-0 No.5065 *Newport Castle* runs alongside the sea wall near Teignmouth with the up train on 14th July 1959. On Mondays to Fridays the train left Kingswear at 11.25am and called at Churston, Paignton and Torquay from where it ran without further booked stops to Exeter St David's. The advertised departure time from the last-mentioned point was at 12.40pm and the 'Torbay Express' then made a non-stop run to Paddington, where its booked arrival time was 3.35pm. The departure times of this train had remained unchanged for many years and those quoted can be traced as far back as 1939!
R. C. Riley

Shap Wells, Barmouth Bridge and the Horseshoe Curve on the West Highland line are all classic photographic locations that have caught the imagination of generations of railway aficionados. But perhaps the most famous of all, and certainly the most popular, is this lovely stretch of the Exeter to Plymouth main line that runs along the sea wall at Teignmouth within a stone's throw of the golden sands. In this shot, dating from the early 1960s, a smartly turned-out 'Hall' Class 4-6-0 No.4955 *Plaspower Hall* ambles along with a westbound train made up of a combination of service vehicles operated by the Civil Engineer's Dept (the first four at the front of the formation) and ordinary goods wagons, most of which appear to be bogie bolsters. Children play on the beach oblivious to the passing train but at least the 'Hall' does seem to have attracted the attention of the two ladies walking along the promenade. *Alan Reeve*

EXETER TO NEWTON ABBOT

A westbound working skirts the river Teign, about three quarters of a mile west of Teignmouth station, on 5th July 1957. Motive power is provided by 'Castle' Class 4-6-0 No.5097 *Sarum Castle*. The train identification number indicates that this is the 9.10am Liverpool Lime Street to Plymouth North Road train and the LMSR-designed coach immediately behind the locomotive certainly indicates that the train is unlikely to have started at Paddington. The exceptional section of line between Exeter and Teignmouth has resulted in this stretch being overshadowed, but between Teignmouth and Newton Abbot there are some lovely views as trains run alongside the northern bank of the river. *R. C. Riley*

The 10.45am Manchester London Road to Plymouth train, with 'Castle' Class 4-6-0 No.4037 *The South Wales Borderers* in charge, runs alongside the placid waters of the Teign estuary, between Teignmouth and Newton Abbot, on 17th July 1959. Part of the town of Teignmouth can just be discerned in the far distance. This locomotive was rebuilt from a 'Star' Class 4-6-0 and remained in service for another three years after this picture was taken. On the Western Region of BR most long distance passenger workings carried a train number for identification purposes and the number displayed on the front of No.4037 enabled the author to identify the train in the photograph. This number represents the last three digits of the train number quoted in the working time table for the 1959 summer service. The official WR operating notice stated that 'stove black plates, with white enamel figures, will be used for slotting into a metal frame carried on the front of the engine'. This equipment may have been a godsend to operating staff but was the object of many caustic comments by train spotters because it obscured an engine's front number plate and, therefore, made identification of individual locomotives much more difficult. *R. C. Riley*

The 1.20pm Paddington to Kingswear is nearing journey's end as it awaits the 'right away' from Newton Abbot on 15th July 1961. The locomotive in charge is No.4704, one of nine 4700 Class 2-8-0s built shortly after the First World War to Churchward's design to work fitted goods services; they were especially associated with the London to Birkenhead route and the West of England main line. They were, however, used as 'mixed traffic' locomotives and these versatile machines were often pressed into service at busy times on long-distance passenger work, and could even be occasionally observed hauling named expresses when the motive power department was really desperate. The photographer commented that No.4704 was hauling thirteen coaches and arrived at Newton Abbot on time, and certainly the driver seems anxious to get a move on! *R. C. Riley*

The 16 miles-long line from Heathfield, on the Moretonhampstead branch, to Exeter St Thomas (City Basin Junction) was opened in stages, the first section from Heathfield to Ashton being brought into use on 9th October 1882. Soon afterwards a short extension to Christow was completed. This route was built to the standard gauge and operated in splendid isolation from the rest of the broad gauge GWR system for ten years until the Moretonhampstead line was converted to standard gauge on 23rd May 1892. The opening of the northern section of the line, from Christow to Exeter through the Haldon hills, was delayed until 1st July 1903 by the very heavy engineering works that were necessary. The complete Heathfield to St Thomas route was known as the Teign Valley line. The train service, at least in latter years, could hardly be described as lavish, the winter 1953 timetable, for example, listing only five 'all stations' trains in each direction along the entire length of the line on Mondays to Fridays, the journey taking roughly an hour. The line's value as a diversionary route between Exeter and Newton Abbot was reduced by its single line status and 1 in 56 gradients. Passenger traffic withered, the passenger service being withdrawn from the entire line on 9th June 1958 while the Christow to Exeter stretch was closed completely. Heathfield station, which was known as 'Chudleigh Road' from its opening on 4th July 1866 until 1st October 1882, is seen in this picture which was taken on 5th March 1961. In times gone by it was the interchange point between the broad gauge Moretonhampstead branch services and standard gauge Teign Valley trains. *John Langford*

Track fast disappearing beneath a carpet of weeds, a semi-derelict station building and a pannier tank locomotive shunting a few wagons completes a scene that does not offer much encouragment for the future of this rural backwater. This is the former Trusham station on 10th August 1961 showing 5700 Class 0-6-0PT No.3659 doing a spot of shunting prior to returning to Newton Abbot with the thrice weekly Teign Valley goods working. After closure to passengers Christow had been the northern limit of operation, but in September 1960 the West Country was affected by some of the worst flooding in living memory and the line north of Trusham was completely washed away, with track left hanging in the air in some places. The goods working depicted here, with No.3659 as motive power, was marooned by floodwater for some days. Trusham, where a concrete-works was located, then became the railhead from Heathfield for a time before it, too, was erased from the railway map. *Hugh Ballantyne*

This really delightful vintage view of Christow station, with a party of young men apparently waiting for a northbound train, was taken in August 1955. Note the rails lying in the 'six foot' between the tracks: presumably some relaying was planned, a sure sign that closure was just around the corner! Following closure to passengers, goods facilities were retained to a quarry at Christow from the Heathfield end, but in September 1960, as previously mentioned, severe flooding washed away the track between Trusham and Ashton and all traffic to Christow ceased. Note the horse and cart in the station forecourt. *The late J.H. Moss / Stuart Ackley collection*

The Moretonhampstead & South Devon Railway Company was authorised on 7th July 1862 to construct a 12½ miles-long line up the valleys of the Teign and Bovey rivers from Newton Abbot to Moretonhampstead. The single, broad gauge line climbed around 500ft and bridges were built to take double track in the expectation that doubling might eventually be necessary, but this was not the case. The line opened on 4th July 1866 and conversion to standard gauge took place between 20th-23rd May 1892. There were originally four intermediate stations between Newton Abbot and Moretonhampstead but, in an effort to attract more custom, the GWR opened new halts at Brimley in 1928 and Hawkmoor in 1931. In the 1930s around fifteen trains were scheduled each way on weekdays but this figure had dwindled to eight by the mid-1950s. Closure to passenger traffic occurred from 2nd March 1959. Photographed on a bright summer day some time in the mid-1950s, Bovey station is depicted in this shot with a 2-6-2T locomotive waiting in the platform. *The late J.H. Moss / Stuart Ackley collection*

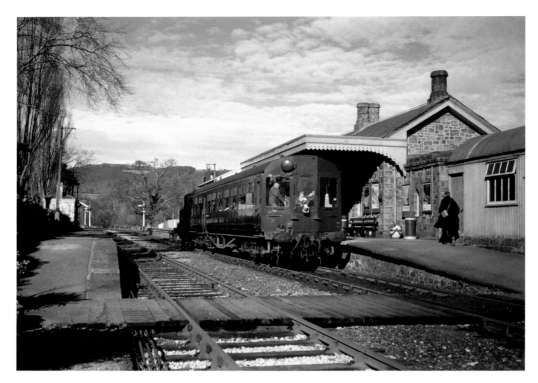

Photographed on 21st February 1959, just a few days before closure to passengers, an auto train is seen at Bovey heading towards Newton Abbot. The train appears to be reasonably well patronised, perhaps due to a number of people making their last, sentimental journey prior to the cessation of passenger services. A local group, the South Devon Railway Society, was formed to campaign for the line's reopening and organised a special train up the branch which ran on Whit Monday, 6th June 1960. This was headed by 5101 Class 2-6-2T No.4174 hauling six coaches carrying about 250 passengers. Further special trains were run in 1961 and 1962. Regrettably, the efforts of the society came to nothing and Devon lost one of its most picturesque branches. *Graham Hoare*

An unidentified southbound train, headed by a nicely cleaned 5101 Class 2-6-2T No.5196, pauses at Lustleigh station on 21st February 1959. Note the road bridge in the background that was built to double track width. The station served a small settlement which nestles in a valley formed by one of the tributaries of the river Bovey and is unlikely to have been busy. No.5196 was built at Swindon in October 1934 and withdrawn in December 1959. *Graham Hoare*

A comprehensive picture, showing most of the railway installations at Moretonhampstead apart from the former engine shed. The main station building, adjacent to the train shed in the middle of the shot, was constructed of local stone and had a slate roof, whilst the train shed was built of timber and braced with wrought iron tie rods. The goods shed was constructed using similar materials to the station building; however, the adjoining corrugated iron shed was added by the GWR at about the time of the Second World War and extended in 1956 to accommodate a local feed merchant. The directors of the Moretonhampstead & South Devon Railway always dreamed of an extension to Chagford and, maybe with this in mind, both tracks were extended a short way beyond the station building. The 'extension' did at least serve the cattle pens which are concealed by the deep shadow to the left of the station. The large field, beyond the fence in the foreground, was used as garden allotments by staff who at one time obviously had plenty to occupy themselves during the long gaps between trains! This picture was also taken on 21st February 1959.
Graham Hoare

The engine shed at Moretonhampstead, depicted here looking southwards in February 1959, was of stone construction and originally had sliding doors which seemed somewhat superfluous on such a small building: they were removed in the late 1940s. Perhaps the engine shed's most unusual feature was the signal box which was built onto the side of it and is partially visible in this photograph. The rather unsightly sheets of corrugated iron on the ventilator replaced the original slate roof at some stage. The shed was closed in about 1948 and after that time branch engines travelled 'light engine' to and from Newton Abbot. *Graham Hoare*

The view from the platform end at Moretonhampstead with the branch goods presumably waiting in the yard for a passenger train to arrive from Newton Abbot. The water tank was fed by gravity from a nearby farm whilst the whitewashed building was the local platelayers' hut. This illustration provides a further view of the engine shed with its adjoining signal box – a most peculiar arrangement. What an idyllic, scenically attractive branch line this must have been! *The late J.H. Moss / Stuart Ackley collection*

MORETONHAMPSTEAD BRANCH

The branch from Newton Abbot to Kingswear was opened in stages, the first section as far as Torre opening on 18th December 1848. The next stretch from Torre to Paignton was brought into use on 2nd August 1859, completion no doubt having being delayed by the need to build twenty bridges, a viaduct and a tunnel which was later opened out. The next three miles, to Churston, followed on 14th March 1861, while the final 3¼ miles to Kingswear were opened on 16th August 1864. This final section was fiercely graded and included heavy engineering works, especially the 495 yards-long Greenway Tunnel. It had been the promoters' intention to take the line to Dartmouth, but this proposal was rejected by Parliament and it was decided that Dartmouth would be best served by a steam ferry from Kingswear, thus creating the most unusual situation where Dartmouth was provided with a station without trains. Torre station was originally served by broad gauge trains and known as 'Torquay' until the line to the present Torquay station was opened in 1859. Goods traffic was handled at Torre from October 1849 but was withdrawn by BR from 4th December 1967. This picture of Torre station's attractive frontage was taken in the 1960s: note the gentleman apparently waiting for a bus, and vintage Royal Mail van. *Gerald Daniels*

Sunny Torquay, or at least Torquay station! A gleaming 'Hall' Class 4-6-0, No.4955 *Plaspower Hall,* pulls out with an unidentified southbound train on 13th October 1961. No.4955 was a Swindon product dating from August 1929 and it remained in service until October 1963. The station was originally opened by the Dartmouth & Torbay Railway on 2nd August 1859 and was worked from the outset by the South Devon Railway, which absorbed the former company in 1872. Torquay station did not have facilities for goods traffic which was dealt with at nearby Torre station. *Colour-Rail*

Northbound trains from Paignton face a short, sharp climb, including a stretch at 1 in 81, before descending towards Torquay and in this picture an immaculately turned-out 'Hall' Class 4-6-0 No.4984 *Albrighton Hall* is clearly exerting maximum effort to keep its train on the move between Paignton and Torquay. The train is the 9.45am Churston to Paddington and this photograph was taken on a very bright and clear 2nd September 1961. The young man standing on the park bench has been rewarded with a superb spectacle, but his dog and the person sitting on the other bench appear to be totally unmoved. Perhaps they had seen it all before! *Colour-Rail*

There is no need to state the location of this picture because the station nameboard is clearly visible on the extreme left. The train does not need any introduction either! This portrait was taken on 13th September 1961 and shows the down working leaving behind 'Castle' Class No.5043 *Earl of Mount Edgcumbe* hauling a uniform rake of Mk.1 coaches in WR 'chocolate and cream' colours. Churston was the junction station for the Brixham branch but this lost its passenger service on 13th May 1963. *Colour-Rail*

NEWTON ABBOT TO KINGSWEAR

Plans to extend the line across the river were thwarted, as previously stated, so Kingswear became the branch terminus. In this picture a nicely turned out 'Hall' Class 4-6-0, No.5992 *Horton Hall,* simmers in Kingswear station with an unidentified passenger working some time in the early 1960s. The station is beautifully situated but on a very restricted site, between the river and the side of the valley, and is completely hidden by the train, but at least the roof of the signal box is just visible above the locomotive. A local double-decker bus, perhaps heading for Brixham or Paignton, adds interest to the scene. *Alan Reeve*

A further picture taken at Kingswear, this time looking in the opposite direction to the previous photograph and showing 'Hall' Class engine, No.4951 *Pendeford Hall,* being turned on the 55ft turntable on 5th August 1961. There was a shed here from 1864 to 1924 and the turntable was doubtless installed as part of the shed's facilities. Kingswear station and its adjacent sidings were built on land reclaimed from the river Dart. Surprisingly, perhaps, there was coal traffic at Kingswear, coasters being unloaded by crane at the jetty by the station. Coal may have been a rather unlikely commodity to be handled in glorious Devon but it was transhipped into waiting trains for the short journey to a local gas works. *Colour-Rail*

An unidentified, double-headed westbound train piloted by 'Hall' Class 4-6-0 No.4976 *Warfield Hall* blasts towards Dainton summit some time in the late 1950s. In steam days the notorious south Devon banks presented a formidable challenge to enginemen, the climb over Dainton summit for Plymouth-bound trains including short stretches as steep as 1 in 36 and 1 in 41. One can only imagine the tremendous noise being made by the two locomotives as the train passed the photographer, probably at little more than walking pace. The crews were no doubt relieved when the summit signal box came into view, but were probably mindful that Rattery bank also had to be surmounted before Plymouth was reached. *Colour-Rail*

There was a gable summit at Dainton, this being a legacy of Brunel's intention to operate the line atmospherically with a pumping house at Dainton. There were two stop boards at the summit applicable to westbound workings, for short or long goods trains, one on each side of the signalbox, and all such trains were obliged to stop to pin down brakes before starting the very steep and tortuous descent towards Totnes. In this picture, however, an eastbound train is depicted, the 11.20am Plymouth to Taunton 'stopper', with smartly turned-out 'Hall' Class 4-6-0 No.6946 *Heatherden Hall* in charge and the photographer comments that, when this shot was taken on 7th August 1961, this working was one of the last remaining main line steam turns in the area. This train was not designed for passengers in a hurry because it stopped at most intermediate stations including wayside places, such as Hele & Bradninch and Burlescombe. The advertised arrival time at Taunton was 2.51pm. *Hugh Ballantyne*

A picture of the east end of Totnes station showing some of the elaborate trackwork that used to be commonplace on the railway system prior to the standardisation of track components for economy reasons. Note the three-way point. The precise date of this illustration is not known but it is believed to have been taken in the mid-1950s. A disastrous fire in the early hours of 14th April 1962 completely gutted the main station buildings on the down platform at Totnes, including the booking office, parcels office and refreshment room. The stock of tickets was destroyed in the conflagration so staff were forced to write out vouchers in lieu of tickets but, it was reported, they had no problems remembering the fares which they knew off by heart! *The late J.H. Moss / Stuart Ackley collection*

The first plans to connect Ashburton with the main line railway system were formulated in 1848 when a group of local promoters proposed a 10½ miles-long line from Newton Abbot. This actually got as far as receiving the Royal Assent and Isambard Kingdom Brunel, who was asked to be the engineer for the project, produced an estimate of £103,500 for its construction. Unfortunately, the economy was in recession at that time and there was little money available for such schemes, with the result that the plan was quietly abandoned. The next landmark in the line's history was the formation of the Buckfastleigh, Totnes and South Devon Railway, which was incorporated in 1864 and gained powers the following year for an extension to Ashburton. The broad gauge line opened for traffic on 1st May 1872. Goods traffic, mainly wool, coal, cider and agricultural equipment, was the lifeblood of the line. Conversion to standard gauge took place during one weekend in May 1892. In the motor age, traffic on the branch was quickly eroded and closure to passengers occurred from 3rd November 1958. Some idea of the sparsity of passenger traffic can be gauged by the fact that on Mondays to Fridays only seven trains were advertised in the winter 1953 timetable. This view from the signal box of the goods shed and part of the station layout at Buckfastleigh (looking towards Totnes) is thought to date from the mid-1950s.
The late J.H. Moss / Stuart Ackley collection

Another view of Buckfastleigh station layout, this time looking towards Ashburton. The tracks on the left were sidings, two of which served cattle docks in the small goods yard. The entire branch was closed to goods traffic from 10th September 1962. The track on the right of the photograph is the down loop.
The late J.H.Moss / Stuart Ackley collection

Taken from the bridge that carries the main Totnes to Buckfastleigh road across the railway, this panoramic view looking southwards to Buckfastleigh station and the surrounding countryside gives an idea of how the station and its immediate environs looked prior to the coming of the preservation society. Two rakes of wagons are prominent, one on each side of the single line, while in the far distance the signal box can just be discerned with the goods shed beyond. There are quite a few wagons in the goods yard together with (what appears to be) a clerestory coach at the end of the far siding. The line between Totnes and Buckfastleigh was reopened by the Dart Valley Railway Company on 5th April 1969, the official opening ceremony being performed by Lord Beeching on 21st May 1969. *The late J.H.Moss / Stuart Ackley collection*

A small group of boys are showing considerable interest in 1400 Class 0-4-2T No.1427 and its train as it waits at Ashburton station on 2nd July 1957. This was a really lovely branch line terminus and it is a great shame that the last two miles of the line to Ashburton were severed by improvements to the A38 trunk road, thus preventing its reopening as the terminus of the preserved Dart Valley line. The last 'ordinary' passenger train along the branch was a Sunday school outing from Buckfastleigh to Teignmouth on 1st August 1962 while the last ever passenger working to Ashburton under BR jurisdiction is thought to have been a brake van special on 8th September organised by the Plymouth Railway Circle, powered by 4500 Class 2-6-2T No.4567 of Plymouth shed. Unfortunately this special train may have been its final working because No.4567 was withdrawn later the same month. In preservation days odd workings up to Ashburton are understood to have operated, the last reportedly being on 2nd October 1971. *R. C. Riley*

Photographed on a glorious spring morning, the 11.57pm (previous day) Manchester Piccadilly to Plymouth train makes a rousing getaway from Totnes behind immaculately turned-out 'Castle' Class 4-6-0 No.5024 *Carew Castle* on 21st May 1961. Unfortunately, judging by the clouds of escaping steam, the locomotive's front end appears to be leaking, but at least it adds a bit more life to the picture! The locomotive is about to tackle the gruelling climb up to Rattery signal box, on gradients ranging from 1 in 47 to 1 in 95. More moderate adverse gradients continue from Rattery to Wrangaton, but once the latter point has been passed the banks are in favour of westbound trains virtually all of the way to Plymouth, so the crew can take things relatively easy. *Gerald Daniels*

The 12½ miles-long branch line from Brent, between Totnes and Plymouth, to the quiet waterfront town of Kingsbridge was a real gem, one of the loveliest lines featured in this album. The main line through Brent was opened by the South Devon Railway on 5th May 1848, but the proposal for a branch line to Kingsbridge was not approved by Parliament until 25th July 1864. Construction was hampered by a shortage of capital – the local populace were apparently unenthusiastic about the prospect of a railway – and work ceased completely after a mere four miles of earthworks had been completed. A new company, the grandly named Kingsbridge & Salcombe Railway Co Ltd, was formed in July 1882 and the line was eventually opened to traffic on 19th December 1893, the local company having been taken over by the GWR in the meantime. The line terminated at Kingsbridge, the proposed extension to Salcombe remaining a pipe dream. In later years traffic was steadily eroded by road transport and the last trains ran on 16th September 1963. In BR days a through train to and from London Paddington ran on summer Saturdays and here the 10.55am SO from Kingsbridge is depicted approaching Brent behind 4575 Class 2-6-2T No.5525 on 5th August 1961 – undoubtedly the branch's crack train of the day! Needless to say the tank locomotive only worked as far as Brent. *Hugh Ballantyne*

The Kingsbridge branch largely followed the course of the meandering river Avon and offered one of the most relaxing and enjoyable journeys one could wish for, with mile after mile of glorious, unspoilt south Devon countryside. One of the prettiest and most beautifully situated stations on the route was Gara Bridge, the only crossing station on the line, which is seen here in this picture looking towards Brent. This shot is thought to have been taken in the mid-1950s. The line crossed over the river on a girder bridge behind the photographer. In later years two camping coaches were stationed at Gara Bridge, undoubtedly a wonderfully idyllic place to stay but one that certainly had its drawbacks. There was nowhere to buy food, which apparently had to be ordered by the signalman and sent up from Kingsbridge by train. Even worse, the camping coaches were not equipped with baths so anyone in need of a bath presumably had to wait for an invitation from a local railwayman or take a quick 'skinny dip' in the river Avon when nobody was around. Clearly, the coaches did not provide much in the way of creature comforts and were promoted with the hardier holiday-maker in mind. But at least they were cheap and the location of many, as here, was simply outstanding.
The late J.H. Moss / Stuart Ackley collection

The Kingsbridge branch took an extremely sinuous route and there was hardly a length of straight track to be found anywhere on the branch. Kingsbridge station was not an exception to this rule as can be seen here in this picture, which is thought to have been taken some time in the 1950s. The principal platform is in the middle of the shot while a bay platform, that was installed when improvements were undertaken in 1916, is on the left. The tiny, granite-built engine shed was tucked away at the end of the bay platform and was equipped with a 12,000-gallon water tank, inspection pit and small coal stage. The main station building, goods shed and the lower part of the signal box were solidly constructed of stone, but the carriage shed (out of sight to the right) was apparently a much later addition. It was merely a corrugated iron shelter painted black and provided accommodation for only two coaches. The substantially-built goods shed had a hand-operated crane and two sheltered loading bays plus a sizeable office. The 'country' end of the station was built on an embankment, this no doubt being a legacy of the promoters' wish to extend the line to Salcombe. Passengers destined for Salcombe were eventually catered for by a GWR bus service that commenced operations on 21st July 1909 and the bus network was later expanded to include Modbury, Dartmouth and Plymouth. *The late J.H. Moss / Stuart Ackley collection*

Photographed on the last day of regular steam working on the branch, 4500 Class 2-6-2T No.4561 waits to leave Kingsbridge with the 7.30pm to Brent on 10th June 1961. A small crowd of onlookers has gathered to witness one of the last scheduled steam trains to depart from the town. The train service along the branch was remarkably static during the entire life of the line, there being about six trains in each direction on Mondays to Fridays with extra workings on Saturdays, including the through London trains previously mentioned. On the freight side, cattle, sugar beet, cider apples, seafood and even rabbits have all been carried at some stage during the line's existence. Some of the trains ran as 'mixed' workings, conveying both passengers and freight traffic. *Michael Allen*

Very few pictures of 'King' Class 4-6-0s were submitted for inclusion in this album, probably due to the fact that the Paddington-West of England expresses were dieselised at an early stage in the BR modernisation programme. Laira shed retained two examples, Nos. 6002 and 6016, until July 1962 when they were transferred to Wolverhampton for the Paddington to Birmingham trains but they did not last long there, being included in a major cull of 'King' class engines – and of WR steam motive power generally – that occurred at the end of the 1962 summer timetable. In this shot, taken on 21st April 1960, No.6024 *King Edward I,* paired with 'Castle' Class No.5098 *Clifford Castle,* tops Hemerdon Bank with the up 'Cornishman' from Penzance to Wolverhampton. *Colour-Rail*

The 11.20am Plymouth to Taunton train, which is depicted in a previous illustration, is seen again, this time climbing Hemerdon Bank with 'Hall' Class No.4970 *Sketty Hall* in charge. As previously stated it was one of the last steam-hauled workings in the area and, therefore, a favourite with photographers. This picture was taken on 8th August 1961. Eastbound trains from Plymouth have to grapple with Hemerdon Bank and the photographer comments that the train seen here was climbing at 1 in 42 which applies for about one and a half miles, the lack of exhaust from the engine being due to the hot weather conditions. Note the various liveries of the coaches forming the train. *Hugh Ballantyne*

An unidentified goods working, largely formed of china clay wagons, makes an interesting sight as it heads westwards near Tavistock Junction, Plymouth, on 29th August 1961. Motive power is provided by 5700 Class 0-6-0PT No.4679 which was built at Swindon in May 1944 and remained in service until May 1965. *R. C. Riley*

4575 Class 2-6-2T No.5572 propels an auto coach towards Plymouth past Laira Junction on 30th August 1961: unfortunately the identity of this train is unknown. This illustration gives a detailed view of the layout at this important junction where tracks to the former Plymouth Friary station (on the extreme right) diverged from the WR main line. The lines in the right foreground gave access to Laira motive power depot. The 4ft 6in gauge Lee Moor Tramway crossed the entire layout on the level just behind the signal box but by the date of this picture most of its track had been removed, apart from a small section which is just visible immediately to the right of the signal box. *R. C. Riley*

Another picture taken at Laira Junction on the same day as the previous shot, this time showing 1361 Class 0-6-0ST No.1363 apparently shunting some coal wagons. In complete contrast to the 5700 Class 0-6-0PT engines, which numbered well over 700 examples, the ranks of the 1361 Class totalled a mere five engines. One of only three classes of outside cylinder 0-6-0T engines ever built by the GWR, the 1361 locomotives were constructed at Swindon Works in 1910, this particular machine being outshopped in June of that year. They were built for use in sidings with very tight curves, weighed 35tons 4cwt and had an 11ft wheelbase. The engine depicted was used for dock shunting purposes while another member of the class was based at Taunton (for use at Bridgwater docks) and other engines were allocated to Swindon. *R. C. Riley*

A comprehensive view of Laira motive power depot which is situated about a mile east of the main Plymouth station, formerly known as Plymouth North Road. This picture dates from July 1960, by which time diesel traction was well in evidence. The photograph illustrates the two principal shed buildings that were built thirty years apart. The brick-built building on the right was opened in 1901 to relieve the congested South Devon Railway shed at Millbay which was originally built way back in 1849. The brick building opposite the shed entrance is the sand shed whilst the depot's hoist and administration offices are just out of the photograph on the right. The depot at Millbay was finally closed in 1931, this loss being compensated for by the construction of a new four-road shed at Laira, known locally as the 'Long Shed', this being seen here on the left of the picture. *R.C. Riley*

BRENT TO PLYMOUTH

A picture of 'Castle' Class 4-6-0 No.7022 *Hereford Castle* apparently being prepared by the crew at Laira shed on 30th April 1961. Maintaining and servicing steam locomotives was always a challenge and on the day of this photograph No.7022's fireman appears to be attempting to break up some huge lumps of coal in the tender, a job where a head for heights and an acrobat's sense of balance are obviously qualifications. In the days of steam many of the enginemen's jobs were laborious, dirty, and sometimes downright dangerous, but for the locomotive crews tasks such as that seen here were simply part of their daily toil.......'health and safety, mate? Never heard of it'. *R. C. Riley*

An atmospheric illustration of the interior of Laira shed on 2nd June 1963 showing 4500 Class 2-6-2T No.4574 apparently stabled between duties. Actually, the locomotive had been withdrawn from service four months previously and was merely awaiting its final journey to a scrap yard. It is recorded that No.4574 was not broken-up until November of the following year so it had a very long wait indeed. Note the interloper on the extreme left – a Bulleid Pacific. This picture graphically portrays the filthy and dilapidated condition of many steam sheds during the dying days of steam traction on BR. In truth, judging by this portrait, Laira appears to have been much tidier than most depots. Despite the dirty and primitive conditions, or maybe because of them, steam sheds had an irresistible appeal to the railway enthusiasts of that time who wallowed in the magical aroma of smoke, steam and oil: a magic that, despite its best efforts, the preservation movement has been unable to recreate convincingly.
Rodney Lissenden

Eastbound trains from Plymouth faced a short, sharp climb, mostly at 1 in 109, to Mutley tunnel before descending towards Laira Junction. In this picture 4575 Class 2-6-2T No.5541 takes the climb in its stride with a lightweight Plymouth to Launceston train on 8th July 1961. At this time Laira shed had an allocation of about ten of these machines mainly for use on the Tavistock and Launceston services. *R. C. Riley*

Despite its undoubted position as one of the busiest stations in Devon, few railway photographers seem to have visited Plymouth station in steam days and even fewer photographed there in colour. Perhaps a station foreman was hostile to railway enthusiasts, but the paucity of pictures is more likely to be explained by the £1,800,000 station rebuilding project which apparently took six years to complete, the premises no doubt resembling a building site for much of this time and hardly conducive to photography. The new station was opened by the late Doctor (later Lord) Beeching on 26th March 1962, by which time the heyday of steam in the city had passed. There is, however, no evidence of building works in this picture of 4575 Class 2-6-2T No.5511 shunting at the east end of the station on 25th September 1960. Perhaps they were digging up the west end at that time! *R. C. Riley*

Few lines in the south west of England could match the dramatic scenery of the Princetown branch, the line climbing to a remarkable altitude of 1,350ft above sea level high up on the wild and desolate heights of Dartmoor. The first railway to reach Princetown was a horse-drawn tramway opened by the Plymouth & Dartmoor Railway (P&DR) in December 1826. This carried passengers and huge quantities of granite from the moor. Many years later the GWR considered constructing a line to Princetown and a deal was struck with the P&DR with the result that a standard gauge line, built almost entirely on the course of the old tramway and with a ruling gradient of 1 in 40, was brought into use on 11th August 1883. There was one intermediate station, Dousland, but three halts were later opened between the wars. The train service, like the population of the area(!), was sparse and generally consisted of six trains each way on weekdays only. The line clearly had little traffic potential and was an early closure casualty, services running for the last time on 5th March 1956. Very few colour pictures of this branch are known to exist and in this shot 4400 Class 2-6-2T No.4410 is seen at Dousland on 5th July 1955. This locomotive was one of eleven engines built in 1904-06 for light branch line duties and was among the last survivors, lasting until August 1955. *R.C. Riley*

Left: The first attempt to promote a line from Plymouth to Tavistock was made in 1844 but this was unsuccessful. A further effort to build a link between those settlements was made, however, and this resulted in the Tavistock & South Devon Railway Act being passed by Parliament on 24th July 1854. The broad gauge line was opened on 22nd June 1859 when, it is recorded, two special trains made the 16 miles-long journey from Plymouth in thirty-seven minutes. The rapid success of the route to Tavistock did not escape the attention of the people of the Cornish town of Launceston and on 30th June 1862 the Launceston & South Devon Railway Act was approved for a line running eastwards to Lydford (then spelt Lidford), on the western fringe of Dartmoor, and then southwards to an end-on junction with the Tavistock & South Devon Railway. This line opened on 1st July 1865. In 1876 the section south of Lydford was converted to dual gauge in order to accommodate LSWR trains, this method of operation continuing until that company opened its own route to Plymouth in 1890. In 1892, however, broad gauge working in the area ceased. This view of Marsh Mills station, opened on 15th March 1861, was taken on 8th July 1961 looking northwards, and shows the china clay works which has always been an important source of railborne traffic. The goods yard here was closed to public traffic from 1st June 1964. An especially interesting feature of the line, at least for a brief period, was near Marsh Mills where the 4ft 6in Lee Moor Tramway crossed the dual gauge branch on the level, giving rise to a very rare three-gauge flat crossing. *R. C. Riley*

Above: A further view of Tavistock South station, taken on 27th June 1964, eighteen months after its closure to passenger traffic. The signal box and water crane are clearly visible on the right of the shot. The section southwards to Plymouth had been closed completely when the passenger service was withdrawn but at the time of this picture the goods yard here was still open for traffic. Strangely, it was served by a daily freight from Okehampton which crossed over to the former GWR branch at Lydford using a wartime connection. This train also served Lifton, near Launceston, where a dairy produced much railborne traffic. This curious working – usually powered by an Ivatt Class 2MT 2-6-2T locomotive – continued until 7th September 1964. *Roy Denison*

Left: A train bound for Plymouth heads away from Tavistock behind 4575 Class 2-6-2T No.5541 on 28th April 1961. After years of decline due to road competition the Plymouth to Launceston line was agreed for closure from 31st December 1962 with the last trains being scheduled to run on Saturday 29th December, there being no Sunday service. On the Saturday afternoon the Plymouth area was hit by a raging blizzard accompanied by 70mph winds and services on the branch were severely affected. The 5.40pm from Launceston, hauled by 2-6-2T locomotive No.4591, managed to struggle through to Marsh Mills but was unable to get onto the main line due to frozen points, and eventually arrived in Plymouth nearly three hours late. Passengers aboard the 6.20pm *ex*-Plymouth, hauled by No.5568 pulling four coaches, fared much worse, however, being delayed by a combination of frozen points and frozen brakes on the train. After passing the 7.10pm Tavistock South to Plymouth, which had been waiting more than three hours to cross the northbound train at Bickleigh, No.5568 reached Tavistock at 12.23am on the Sunday morning having taken over five hours to cover the 15³/₄ miles from Plymouth. Twenty-five passengers were forced to spend the night on the train and were taken on by road the following morning, the line by this time being totally blocked at Lydford due to drifting snow and the telegraph wires being out of action. Fifteen diehard railway enthusiasts who had travelled on the 6.20pm tried to get back to Plymouth from Tavistock North station on a train from Waterloo, but this had become stuck at Bridestowe and it was Sunday lunchtime before they returned home. Meanwhile, at Bickleigh three passengers off the 7.10pm Tavistock to Plymouth train spent the night in the signal box after the locomotive ran out of water. This train was rescued the following day, twenty hours after its arrival, and became the last passenger service on the branch. So, the final weekend of passenger trains on the route will long be remembered – but not for the usual reasons! *John Beckett*

An auto-train bound for Plymouth, propelled by 6400 Class 0-6-0PT No.6430, awaits departure at Tavistock South station in August 1962. This station was originally the terminus of the Tavistock & South Devon Railway and was by far the most important intermediate station on the branch. It was provided with a substantial train shed that spanned two platforms and three tracks. The original buildings were built of wood but these were destroyed by fire in 1887 and replaced by a stone structure located on the platform used by trains bound for Plymouth. There was a footbridge at the north end of the premises. On 26th September 1949 BR renamed the station 'Tavistock South' while the town's other station, on the former Southern Region Okehampton to Plymouth route, became 'Tavistock North'. *Alan Reeve*

PLYMOUTH TO LAUNCESTON

The western fringe of Dartmoor is visible on the horizon as 4500 Class 2-6-2T No.4574 ambles downhill at the approach to Brentor with a southbound goods train, presumably from Launceston, in August 1962. This locomotive was built at Swindon in November 1924 and lasted in traffic until February 1963. The double track line visible on the right is the former London & South Western Railway (LSWR) Okehampton to Plymouth route. When the standard gauge Okehampton to Lydford line was opened in October 1874 passengers bound for Plymouth were forced to change onto the Launceston-Plymouth broad gauge trains until the section south of Lydford was converted to mixed gauge in 1876. The LSWR were unhappy with these arrangements, however, especially following the derailment of one of its locomotives between Yelverton and Bickleigh, and vowed to obtain an independent route from Lydford to Plymouth, which opened on 31st May 1890. Thus as a result of rivalry between the companies two lines ran virtually parallel through the very lightly trafficked area from Lydford to Tavistock. Perhaps if the development of the railway system had been better co-ordinated at that time one of them might still be in operation today! *Alan Reeve*

The local landmark of Brent Tor church stands out on the horizon as 4500 Class 2-6-2T No.4555 enters Lydford with the 10.25am Plymouth to Launceston train, which seems to be assured of picking up at least one passenger! This shot was taken on 23rd June 1962. Note the wide space between the tracks indicating the line's broad gauge origins. Incredibly, the small village of Lydford, which was located around 600ft above sea level, was actually served by two stations, the former SR station being just out of sight on the left of the photograph, though it should be pointed out that the up SR Okehampton and down WR Plymouth platforms were adjoined. *R. C. Riley*

PLYMOUTH TO LAUNCESTON

There were a number of small halts on the Plymouth to Launceston line such as Plym Bridge, Shaugh Bridge and Whitchurch Down, all of which were opened in 1906/7. For reasons unknown to the author these small stations were officially called 'platforms', rather than halts, but to add to the confusion other small stations on the route were known as halts! On 4th April 1938 another tiny station was brought into use, this time to serve the small hamlet of Liddaton, and in this picture 4575 Class 2-6-2T No.5544 is seen coming to a stand to pick up a lady passenger some time in the early 1960s. A simple wooden platform was provided here together with a wooden waiting shelter. The thickly wooded slopes of Longham Down are prominent on the left while Dartmoor forms a distant, hazy backdrop. *R. C. Riley*

Left: Beautifully framed by overhanging branches, the 3.05pm Plymouth to Launceston train, headed by 4500 Class 2-6-2T No.4574, pulls away from its Coryton station stop on a rather overcast 10th September 1962. The building in the background is presumably the former stationmaster's house. Note that the tiny goods yard, entrance to which was controlled by the ground frame on the right, appears to contain two wagons carrying containers. *John Beckett*

Below: Between Tavistock and Launceston the line passed through some very sparsely populated countryside, the only places of any significance being the villages of Lydford and Lifton. Here, in this portrait of the pretty little station at Coryton taken on 23rd June 1962, the emptiness of the surrounding countryside is clearly apparent. A lady passenger waits for the next train on the sole platform seat provided. Obviously, traffic levels here did not warrant the provision of two seats. The station at Coryton, which was provided from the opening of the line in 1865, became unstaffed from 14th September 1959. Note the brightly-painted telephone booth, GWR cast iron notice on the chimney breast and ornate platform lamp. *R. C. Riley*

A view of Lifton station, taken on a damp 15th September 1962, showing 4575 Class No.5545 simmering in the up platform with a short freight train. Despite being a small and remote station Lifton was actually a major source of goods traffic on the Plymouth to Launceston line. A corn mill was opened here way back in 1894 and in 1917 a factory was established that handled milk traffic and manufactured rice puddings. Following closure of the Plymouth to Launceston branch to passengers, Lifton continued to be served for a time by a goods service operated from Okehampton via Lydford. All services to Lifton ceased, however, from 28th February 1966. *Michael Allen*

A portrait of Launceston shed on 2nd May 1961: at the time of this picture it was a sub-shed of Plymouth (Laira). The stone-built shed was constructed in 1865 and remained little changed throughout its life apart from lengthening in 1899. It was located on the northern fringe of the town which accounts for the fact that there are no other buildings in the shot. The tracks in the foreground are those of the North Cornwall Line. *R. C. Riley*

A train for Plymouth, with 4575 Class No.5569 in charge, awaits departure from the former SR Launceston station on 4th July 1959. The town was originally served by the GWR Plymouth branch, which used Launceston (North) station, while trains on the SR North Cornwall Line had their own separate premises – a typical case of gross over-provision! From 1st January 1951 the premises depicted here were known as 'Launceston (South)', but in June 1952 common sense finally prevailed when the old GWR station was closed to passenger traffic and services diverted to the SR station, which was known simply as 'Launceston' once again. Hence the old LSWR concrete running-in board in this picture! During the Second World War the government feared that heavy damage might be inflicted by German bombers on the railway network around Plymouth and in 1943 a connection was laid between the two lines to provide as much operational flexibility as possible. When goods traffic was withdrawn from the Okehampton to Wadebridge line a section of the GWR route from Lifton (then the terminus of a goods only branch from Lydford) to Launceston, which had been closed completely, was reopened from 7th September 1964. *Roy Patterson*

Isambard Kingdom Brunel's masterpiece – the Royal Albert Bridge, Saltash. The river is 1,100ft wide and 70ft deep at this point and the Admiralty required a high-water clearance of 100ft. Excavations had established that there was deep sand and mud on the riverbed, and Brunel soon discarded plans both for a timber bridge with numerous spans and a four-span bridge which would have needed four piers. The idea of a single-span bridge was also rejected as being too costly, so the structure that was finally agreed upon was, therefore, something of a compromise. Each of the main spans is 455ft in length, with seven approach spans on the Devon side and ten on the Cornish side. The principal spans were put together on site and floated out into the river, and then gradually raised into position by jacks while the supporting piers were being built. It was originally envisaged that the bridge would carry double track but a saving of £100,000 was made by reducing its capacity to a single line. The bridge, which cost £225,000, was officially opened by Prince Albert on 2nd May 1859 and public traffic began two days later. In 1959 the bridge celebrated its centenary and BR entered into the spirit of the occasion by removing the ladders and platforms on the end towers that give access to the interior of the tubes. This ensured that the lettering on the towers was uncluttered and clearly visible, as seen here in this picture that was taken in May 1959. In addition, the main structure was also illuminated at night. Note the former LSWR line to Bere Alston and Okehampton on the opposite bank and that work on the new road bridge had not yet commenced. *The late J.H. Moss / Stuart Ackley collection*

During the centenary celebrations for the Royal Albert Bridge, Saltash station was especially decorated (some might say, disguised) to mark the occasion. There are no prizes for guessing the identity of the gentleman depicted on the left! Completion of the bridge enabled the line from Plymouth to Truro to be officially opened throughout to passenger traffic, but it is understood that passengers had been carried unofficially on the western section of the line for some weeks prior to opening. *The late J. H. Moss / Stuart Ackley collection*

The opening of the new road bridge in October 1961 immediately made the Saltash auto trains redundant, not to mention, of course, the chain ferry across the river Tamar. Both had provided yeoman service for many years and provided a vital link between Devon and Cornwall: henceforth travel between the two counties would be much quicker and more convenient but not nearly so interesting. In this picture part of the new bridge is visible in the background as 6400 Class 0-6-0PT No.6400 awaits departure from Saltash station with one of the few trains that ran through to Tavistock. This shot was taken on 28th August 1961, shortly before the auto trains were withdrawn. No.6400 was the first of its class to be constructed, being outshopped from Swindon works in February 1932: it lasted in service until April 1964. *R. C. Riley*

PLYMOUTH TO LISKEARD

A vintage colour view of St Germans station, believed to date from August 1955. The main line west of Plymouth twists and turns, as exemplified here, and was definitely not designed for speed. The original Cornwall Railway single line between Saltash and St Germans ran much more closely to the bank of the Lynher river, but was constructed on a new alignment when it was doubled by the GWR in 1908. In addition to 'ordinary' main line services, St Germans station was also served by a few 'odd' auto trains from Plymouth such as (in the 1961 summer timetable) the 12.05pm to Menheniot which formed the 12.49pm return service. *The late J.H. Moss / Stuart Ackley collection*

Trunks, cases, mailbags, boxes and barrows are strewn across Liskeard's up platform in a higgledy-piggledy fashion as 'Grange' Class 4-6-0 No.6824 *Ashley Grange* runs into the down platform with a Penzance-bound train. Presumably all of the passengers' luggage, not to mention the Post Office's 'luggage', was waiting to be loaded onto an up train for which the passengers are waiting. Note the gas lighting, dainty overhead signal and the tightly curved connection to the Looe branch platform, which is out of sight on the left of the picture. This shot was taken on 30th April 1959. *Colour-Rail*

A further view of Liskeard station, this time taken on 12th August 1960, looking eastwards from a conveniently positioned road bridge that straddles the station. The station footbridge is in the foreground whilst the signal box and water tower are prominent features in the middle of the picture; between them lies the connection to the Looe branch platform. The signal box dates from June 1915, when it replaced the original box which was located on the up platform. The goods yard and shed occupied a site at the country end of the station, on the up side, but the goods facility was withdrawn from 16th December 1963. The parapets of Liskeard viaduct, on which the Looe branch is crossed, are visible just beyond the signals while in the distance the four arches Bolitho viaduct, which carries the railway across a tributary of the Looe river, can be seen. When the line was built there were thirty-four viaducts between Saltash and Truro. The sinuous nature of the Plymouth to Truro line, previously mentioned, is clearly apparent from this picture. Liskeard station, with its peculiar, unorthodox 'right-angled' layout, is one of the most distinctive in Great Britain, and certainly the most interesting station included in this album. *Roy Denison*

The history of the 8¾ miles-long branch from Liskeard to Looe is quite eventful and can be traced back as far as 28th November 1844 when the Liskeard & Caradon Railway was opened from Moorswater, situated in a valley below Liskeard, to South Caradon, on the fringe of Bodmin Moor. The purpose of this line, which was built as standard gauge with rails laid on granite blocks, was to convey tin ore and granite to the basin of the Liskeard & Looe Union canal at Moorswater where it was transhipped. In March 1846 an extension to Cheesewring quarry was brought into use. Loaded trucks descended by gravity and were returned empty by horses. The line prospered and when traffic reached 40,000 tons annually it was extended to Looe along the banks of the Looe river, thus creating the Liskeard & Looe railway, this opening on 27th December 1860. It should, however, be noted that at this time the line conveyed only goods traffic but passengers were carried in open wagons. The Looe line commenced orthodox passenger operations on 11th September 1879 but there was no connection with the main line until the GWR installed a loop between Coombe Junction (where reversal was necessary) and Liskeard station which opened in May 1901. This quite sharply curved and extremely steeply graded connection forms a spectacular spiral which provides passengers with a particularly interesting and memorable journey. Looe branch trains use a separate platform at Liskeard that is at right angles to the main line station. The GWR took over both the Caradon and Looe lines in 1909 but the Caradon system was abandoned in 1916; however, the Looe branch proved to be a great survivor, due to the inability of buses to reach some of the scattered communities it serves, and it remains very much in use today. In this view large puffy clouds scud across the sky as a 4575 Class 2-6-2T locomotive awaits departure from Liskeard on 12th August 1960. *Roy Denison*

The small engine shed at Moorswater, seen here in August 1960, was probably in the most idyllic location of any in Cornwall, but perhaps it should be pointed out that the A38 main road ran through the trees here so this spot may not have been quite as peaceful as it appears. The shed was originally the locomotive and carriage & wagon workshops for the Liskeard & Looe and Liskeard & Caradon railways, which made an end-on junction here, and is thought to have been constructed in around 1861. When the GWR took over operation of the two lines in 1909 it was retained to house the engines working on the Looe branch. Latterly it was a sub-shed of St Blazey. *Roy Denison*

An illustration of the small halt at Coombe Junction, also taken in August 1960, looking towards Looe. Note the decidedly basic facilities provided for passengers, merely a small waiting shelter, a single platform seat and an oil lamp. The line behind the photographer led to Moorswater engine shed. All trains have to reverse here and in steam days this was accomplished in a very slick and efficient manner, doubtless with the locomotive making a considerable amount of noise as it fussily moved from one end of the train to the other – just the kind of performance that made the study of railways such great fun for the enthusiast. This delightful method of working would have been lost if the GWR's plan for a new suburban railway serving Plymouth had materialised. It envisaged a completely new branch line from St Germans to East Looe, the terminus being conveniently close to a new GWR hotel that was being planned. A commuter service from Plymouth was proposed, apparently using diesel railcars, but the scheme involved three tunnels and a viaduct which probably explains why it never came to fruition. *Roy Denison*

This tiny halt is situated 3³/₄ miles from Liskeard and serves the small hamlet of St Keyne, which is almost a mile to the west. The station nameboard proclaimed 'St Keyne For St Keyne Well', the well, which is presumably a small local attraction, being located just over half a mile away. This shot was taken looking northwards in August 1960. The Looe river is just out of sight on the left. The stone bridge takes a local lane across the railway and also crosses a small tributary of the Looe river which runs along the former canal bed. It incorporates two different styles, indicating it was originally built as a bridge across the canal and later extended when the line was constructed. *Roy Denison*

The guard has just jumped aboard the 10.35am train from Liskeard to Looe and 4500 Class 2-6-2T No.4574 is ready to set off from Sandplace Halt on the last stage of its journey to the terminus. This picture was taken on 13th August 1961. A trip along the Looe branch offers one of the most enjoyable and relaxing journeys one could wish for, with a constantly changing vista from the carriage window. The hills in the background give a hint of the appealing landscape through which the line passes. *Roy Patterson*

The branch terminus at Looe is depicted in this portrait which was taken on 20th August 1959, with 4500 Class 2-6-2T No.4565 in the platform after arrival with a train from Liskeard. A lady sitting on the platform seat appears to be momentarily distracted by the photographer! It may not be immediately apparent from the picture, but Looe station is sandwiched between the main road, on the right, and the Looe river which is much wider at this point than the small stream that runs parallel to the line for most of the way from Coombe Junction. At the time this photograph was taken the railway sidings extended for some distance along the river bank all of the way down to the road bridge between East and West Looe. In times gone by they served Looe quay where boats were loaded with ores and granite. *Alan Jarvis*

Few stations in Cornwall (or, arguably, in Great Britain) have quite the appeal of Bodmin General, without doubt a really attactive and compact station, and a railway modeller's dream subject. It has the ambience of a branch line terminus but, in reality, it was not the end of the line, merely an intermediate station between Bodmin Road and Wadebridge where locomotives ran-round their trains before resuming their journey. The line coming in from Bodmin Road is in the middle of the shot whilst the Wadebridge track is on the left. Regrettably, the station was robbed of much of its charm when the demolition of the engine shed, goods shed and signal box was quite needlessly ordered by BR's architectural Philistines – a sad day indeed. Today, the station enjoys a new lease of life as the headquarters of the Bodmin & Wenford Railway. This photograph was taken on 16th May 1960. *R. C. Riley*

A train from Bodmin General eases around the tight curve into Bodmin Road station (now known as Bodmin Parkway) behind 4575 Class 2-6-2T No.5518 on 26th April 1962. The tracks of the Plymouth to Penzance main line are visible in the foreground. Today the sight and sound of a steam train can still be experienced at Bodmin Parkway station as a result of the efforts of the preserved Bodmin & Wenford Railway. *John Beckett*

A view of Nanstallon Halt, between Wadebridge and Boscarne Junction, taken on 19th March 1966. At first sight it might be assumed that the halt, with its typical pagoda shelter, was of GWR origin but it was actually opened by the LSWR, who had taken over from the Bodmin & Wadebridge Railway, on 2nd July 1906 in connection with the introduction of a railmotor service between Wadebridge and Bodmin North. Originally, it was of timber construction with no shelter of any kind, the pagoda presumably being a much later addition. There was a siding at Nanstallon Halt but this was closed from 2nd May 1960. *Roy Patterson*

A scene at Wadebridge recorded on 22nd June 1962 showing 1366 Class 0-6-0PT No.1368 shunting Maunsell-designed passenger stock. At the time of this photograph the ancient Beattie well tank locomotives were still in charge of mineral trains to and from Wenfordbridge, but there were plans to replace them and No.1368 had been sent from Weymouth to evaluate the suitability of the class on the lightly laid and tightly curved branch. The trials were successful and other members of the class later arrived with the result that the reign of the Beattie engines ended in August 1962. The 1366 Class locomotives were not destined to last for long on these workings, however, because dieselisation was proceeding apace in Cornwall and their duties were taken over by a diesel shunter in September 1964. *R. C. Riley*

The signalman in Wadebridge East box holds out the token to the crew of 4575 Class 2-6-2T No.5573 as it leaves with a train to Bodmin Road on 1st August 1961. Workings under the auspices of the Bodmin & Wadebridge Railway commenced operation along the wooded valley of the river Camel from Wadebridge towards Bodmin (later 'Bodmin North') way back in 1834. They were the first steam hauled trains in the county, conveying predominately sea-sand, china clay and granite, the pioneering stretch from Wadebridge to Dunmere opening on 4th July 1834 whilst the Dunmere to Bodmin/Wenfordbridge sections opened on 30th September of the same year. Bodmin (General) to Bodmin Road, on the main line from the West Country to London, was a much later arrival on the scene, not opening until 27th May 1887. On 3rd September 1888 a link was opened from Bodmin General to the Wadebridge line at what became known as Boscarne Junction. *Colour-Rail*

The palm trees on the platforms give Lostwithiel an almost Mediterranean air in this photograph which was taken looking eastwards on 8th August 1960. The station's appearance is further enhanced by the circular flowerbeds with their neat stone surrounds. The footbridge, signal box and crossing gates are visible at the far end of the station together with the inevitable line-up of platform barrows on the up platform. The train on the right is a Fowey branch working. Branch trains left the station on their own independent track and sometimes a 'race' would take place with a simultaneous departure on the main line. There is a bank of sidings behind the train for china clay traffic. Beyond the signal box there are up and down goods loops, these being installed in 1943 and 1936 respectively. *Roy Denison*

LOSTWITHIEL STATION

The Lostwithiel & Fowey Railway obtained an Act of Parliament on 30th June 1862 to open a broad gauge goods-only line between the towns and this was opened for traffic on 1st June 1869, its main traffic being china clay. The line terminated at Carne Point, about a mile short of Fowey. The opening of a rival route from St Blazey, near Par, to Fowey by the Cornwall Minerals Railway (which also carried china clay) on 1st June 1874 led to a price war with the result that the Lostwithiel & Fowey Railway ceased operations from 1st January 1880. The company was dissolved by Act of Parliament and transferred to the Cornwall Minerals Railway with the result that the line was relaid as a standard gauge route and a connection installed to link the two railways, thus enabling trains from Lostwithiel to run into Fowey. The line reopened on 16th September 1895 conveying both passenger and goods traffic for the first time. A passenger service originally operated between St Blazey and Fowey but this was discontinued from 8th July 1929 leaving just a few services for workmen until they, too, were taken off at the end of 1934. In August 1968 this line was converted to a road as a result of an agreement between BR and English China Clays Ltd. Passenger trains survived on the line from Lostwithiel until 4th January 1965 but the china clay trains continue to operate. In this illustration 1400 Class 0-4-2T No.1419 waits in the bay platform at Fowey with a train to Lostwithiel as a 'Warship' diesel locomotive passes through the station with a train of empty china clay wagons from the jetties beyond the station. This photograph was taken on 22nd July 1960. *R. C. Riley*

A further picture at Fowey, this time looking towards St Blazey on 8th July 1955. This shot illustrates the very sinuous nature of the exit from Fowey station. The locomotive depicted is, once again, No.1419 which was the regular branch engine for most of the 1950s. The branch was converted to diesel multiple unit operation from 17th April 1961, a single unit railcar sufficing for the modest amount of traffic on offer. 1400 Class 0-4-2T No.1468 reportedly worked the last steam trains. *R. C. Riley*

FOWEY BRANCH

The history of the Par to Newquay line can be traced as far back as 1842 when a local landowner and industrialist, J.T.Treffry Esq., opened a mineral line from Ponts Mill (near St Blazey) to Bugle. This included an absolutely magnificent combined viaduct and aqueduct across the Luxulyan valley. In 1849 he opened a similar line from Newquay harbour to St Dennis which crossed the Trenance valley on a timber viaduct that was later replaced by a more substantial stone structure. In 1873 the Cornwall Minerals Railway (CMR) was authorised to build a line from Fowey to Newquay using parts of the old mineral lines and this was opened for regular goods traffic on 1st June 1874. This line took a different course from the bottom of the Luxulyan valley rather than crossing it on a viaduct, albeit at the cost of heavy gradients. In 1876 the impoverished CMR started a passenger service between Fowey and Newquay to compensate for the loss of china clay traffic which was in decline at that time. In 1879 the GWR laid a connection between St Blazey and Par, thus completing the Newquay branch as it is known today. In this picture 5700 Class 0-6-0PT No.8702 passes St Blazey with a Newquay to Par train on 20th July 1960. The CMR built an extensive works and engine shed at St Blazey which was the 'nerve centre' of railway operations in the area. *R. C. Riley*

Above: Regrettably, no photographs of the impressive combined viaduct and aqueduct across the Luxulyan valley were submitted for inclusion in this album but here is the next best thing – a shot taken from the viaduct looking down on the railway. This depicts (what appears to be) a local train heading up the thickly wooded valley towards Newquay in the early 1960s. A very stiff 1 in 39 gradient applied at this point and the heaviest summer Saturday holiday trains, which could load to twelve coaches, sometimes required three locomotives – two at the front and one banking – to heave them up the bank. One can only imagine the deafening noise and thick smoke that filled the valley. A 'Hall' Class locomotive, for example, was only permitted to take 190 tons up the bank without assistance. This line partly replaced the original mineral tramway which incorporated an incline at Carmears, near Ponts Mill, but the viaduct continued to carry granite from Colcerrow quarry to Luxulyan until about 1930.
R. C. Riley

Right: A relic of a lost age. This splendid vintage road sign was still *in situ* near Roche station in 1974, when this photograph was taken. *Gerald Daniels*

Between Roche and St Columb Road the railway crosses the wild and desolate expanse of Goss Moor, where it runs parallel to the A30 main road, before reaching St Dennis Junction. This really vintage view of the junction shows 5700 Class 0-6-0PT No.9673 approaching with a Par to Newquay train in July 1955. The 'main line' tracks are on the left whilst those on the right beyond the junction led (from left to right) to a railway tip, Drinnick Mill and Meledor Mill. The last-mentioned line is, however, only partially visible. Huge waste tips from the china clay workings dot the skyline, giving a hint of the lunar landscape which makes this part of Cornwall so distinctive. The network of goods-only lines converging on St Dennis Junction was gradually whittled away, the line to Parkandillack closing in February 1966 while the section to Meledor Mill was shut in April 1982. The signal box was closed on 14th December 1986. *R. C. Riley*

The 1.30pm train to Truro waits to leave Platform One at Newquay station on 11th June 1961. This working would have been routed via Perranporth along a route long since closed. Motive power is 4575 Class 2-6-2T No.5509 which was withdrawn from traffic a few months after this shot was taken. The GWR was prominent in developing holiday traffic to the Cornish resorts and introduced through carriages from London to Newquay in May 1906. The GWR's efforts were so successful that the relatively short platforms at Newquay were unable to cope and Platform One was progressively extended between the wars. The burgeoning holiday traffic resulted in all of the platforms being extended in 1946 and by the late-1950s up to twelve full-length trains, some double-headed, were booked to leave Newquay between Friday evening and Saturday afternoon. When the CMR constructed its line across Goss Moor in the 1870s they would have had little idea of the very heavy holiday passenger traffic that would later develop to this popular resort. *Michael Allen*

An authentic vintage colour picture of GWR steam at Truro or a digitally manipulated image? Readers may be forgiven for scratching their heads, but this picture is quite genuine and was actually taken on 22nd July 1960 showing 4500 Class 2-6-2T No.4549 taking water at the country end of the station. The GWR number on the buffer beam was reportedly the handiwork of an enthusiastic fireman at Launceston, who was clearly a talented painter, and not a legacy of pre-nationalisation ownership. The fate of the BR front number plate has not been disclosed! This locomotive had previously been allocated to Laira but was based at Truro at the time of this picture. *R. C. Riley*

Another picture at the western end of Truro station. A pair of pannier tank engines waits in the down bay apparently at the head of a passenger train to Falmouth. The provision of two locomotives for a Falmouth branch 'local' may seem excessive at first sight but it is likely one of the engines was on an unbalanced working or *en route* to Falmouth for shunting duty. The leading locomotive is 5700 Class 0-6-0PT No.5744 which was running without a proper chimney. Earlier in its career this engine (together with No. 3709 depicted on page 99) had been fitted with a spark arresting chimney for working at the Ministry of Defence depot at Didcot, but when the locomotive was transferred to Truro crews found that this device affected its steaming and it was removed, leaving only the chimney liner and this resulted in a rather peculiar looking machine. This photograph was taken on 29th April 1961. *R. C. Riley*

The West Cornwall Railway (WCR) opened its line from Penzance to Redruth on 11th March 1852 and an extension to Truro Road station, on the outskirts of Truro, was brought into use on 25th August of the same year. Three years later the WCR completed a new Truro terminus at Newham but this was extremely short-lived, passenger traffic ceasing in May 1859 when the WCR was able to use the main Truro station. Newham's career as a passenger terminus may have been brief but its life as a goods-only depot was precisely the opposite and it was still busy when this portrait of 4575 Class 2-6-2T No.5552 shunting at the former terminus was taken on 20th July 1960. The Truro river and city's outstanding cathedral form a fascinating backdrop. *R. C. Riley*

The 11¾ miles-long branch from Truro to Falmouth was originally planned as part of the Cornwall Railway's route from Plymouth which was authorised by Parliament on 3rd August 1846. The broad gauge line from Plymouth to Truro opened to traffic on 2nd May 1859 while the extension to Falmouth was brought into use on 24th August 1863. An extension to Falmouth docks was laid and brought into use in January 1864. The Falmouth branch crosses a number of valleys and construction was bedevilled by many viaducts and two tunnels that had to be constructed. A total of eight timber viaducts was built but four of these were eventually replaced by embankments. The last timber viaduct was Collegewood (318 yards long and 100 ft high) and this lasted until July 1934. The first station on the branch for Falmouth-bound services was Perranwell, which was known as 'Perran' for the first few months of its existence, and its splendid 21-lever signal box of 1894 vintage is prominent in this view that probably dates from the early 1960s. The box remained in use until 18th April 1966 when the up sidings and loop were removed. The goods yard closed to general traffic in 1965 but occasional flower and sugar beet consignments continued for some time thereafter.
The late J.H. Moss / Stuart Ackley collection

A Truro to Falmouth train, hauled by 5700 Class 0-6-0PT locomotive No.3709, leaves the intermediate station of Penryn on 3rd June 1961. In 1922 work was undertaken at Penryn to reduce track curvature and provide more siding space. The squat building with two white chimneys just discernible on the extreme right is the original station building and gives a good idea of the previous alignment. *John Beckett*

A general view of Falmouth station on a gloomy day some time in the early 1960s. Originally, the station here had arrival and departure platforms, these being on the right and left of the picture respectively. Note that the arrival platform is much longer than the one used for departures. In the late-1920s the GWR rearranged the signalling so that the arrival platform could be used for departing services, this no doubt making the station much easier to work. At one time the station boasted an impressive overall roof, but this disappeared in the early 1950s. The station area was controlled by a 41-lever signal box until it was closed in February 1966. Falmouth never achieved its potential as a port, perhaps due to its remoteness from the main population centres, but at least the GWR did much to promote its attributes as a holiday resort.
The late J.H. Moss / Stuart Ackley collection

The 2.20pm Truro to Penzance semi-fast train runs into Chacewater station behind 'Grange' Class 4-6-0 No.6870 *Bodicote Grange* on 11th June 1961. Chacewater was the junction for the Perranporth and Newquay line trains which used the loop platform on the left of the shot and then ran independently of the main line until they turned off towards the coast. The first railway in this part of the world was the Redruth & Chasewater mineral line opened in 1825 but, ironically, the Newquay branch was a very late arrival on the scene, not being opened throughout until 1905. *Michael Allen*

Unlike the vast majority of lines in this volume that were originally planned by local companies, the 18½ miles-long Chacewater to Newquay line was opened by the GWR. The first section, from Chacewater, on the Plymouth to Penzance main line, to Perranporth carried its first passengers on 6th July 1903 while the remaining stretch to Newquay was brought into use on 2nd January 1905. It was the final passenger route to be built in Cornwall. Construction of this line put paid to any lingering territorial ambitions the LSWR may have had in this part of the county. Originally the convergence with the main line at Chacewater consisted of an elaborate double track triangular junction at Blackwater with three signal boxes which gave direct access to Newquay from the Redruth direction. Later, common sense prevailed and this layout was abandoned in favour of a third track laid alongside the main line into Chacewater station, a much simpler and cheaper arrangement. The line was noted for its abundance of 'Pagoda' halts, while almost all of the larger stations had an unusual island platform layout. Shepherds station, photographed from a passing train on 21st August 1959, was an exception, however, being the only crossing station on the branch to have conventional side platforms. The section from Shepherds to Newquay followed the course of the old Newquay to East Wheal Rose mineral line which could be traced as far back as 1849. The Chacewater to Newquay route was a distinctive line with a fascinating history so it is a pity that it was closed on 4th February 1963 – a sad loss. *Alan Jarvis*

Perranporth station, with trains passing, is seen in this picture which was taken on 9th August 1960. Note the interesting island platform layout that was, as previously mentioned, a feature of this branch. The last trains ran on Saturday 2nd February 1963, there being no Sunday service at that time, and it was reported that some of the last day revellers had actually travelled on the first train! This, of course, was not beyond the realms of possibility because the line was a mere sixty years old and, regrettably, had a brief existence. *Roy Denison*

A further shot of Perranporth station with a train from Newquay, headed by 4575 Class 2-6-2T No.5537, in the platform. This picture was taken on 23rd September 1960. In the summer 1961 timetable nine Monday to Friday trains were advertised between Truro and Newquay (ten in the opposite direction) whilst on Saturdays an extra return train was provided, presumably for the benefit of holiday-makers. In addition to the local service on Saturdays there was an 8.15am Perranporth to London Paddington train which was timetabled to reach the capital at 3.55pm. In the reverse direction the train departed from London at 8.25am and was due in Perranporth at 4.20pm. On Sundays six trains (seven in the down direction) ran along the entire length of the line, these being supplemented by one or two short workings to Perranporth from each end of the line. *R. C. Riley*

Gwinear Road station was built purely because, when the Helston branch was being planned, it was the most convenient junction point with the main line and was not expected to generate much originating traffic of its own. In fact, like some other well-known junction stations, such as Riccarton and Dovey, the station was very much 'out in the wilds' with few houses in the vicinity, and in any case alternatives to Gwinear Road were available not too far away at Camborne and Hayle. Despite its isolation, the station's junction status necessitated the laying of sidings on the down side of the main line, these being visible in the background of this illustration which shows 'Grange' Class 4-6-0 No.6868 *Penrhos Grange* entering with the 4.20pm Truro to Penzance train on 26th May 1962. The single line to Helston is on the right of the shot. A quiet country lane crossed over the railway at this point and required the substantial level crossing gates seen in the foreground; it was an unusual case of the railway part of the crossing being apparently more than twice the width of the road. The station was opened under the auspices of the West Cornwall Railway on 11th March 1852. Passenger services were withdrawn from 5th October 1964 while goods services continued to be provided until 9th August 1965. *Roy Patterson*

The other end of Gwinear Road station. Passengers with heavy luggage – presumably homegoing holiday-makers – line the up platform on Saturday 2nd September 1961 as 'Grange' Class No.6836 *Estevarney Grange* runs in with an unidentified up train. The line through Gwinear Road formed part of the West Cornwall Railway's Redruth to Penzance route and the initial passenger service consisted of three daily trains. The line was built to the standard gauge (sometimes referred to as 'narrow gauge' when compared to broad gauge) but it was stipulated that the line's civil engineering works should be sufficiently wide to take broad gauge trains. In the event broad gauge goods trains commenced running to Penzance on 6th November 1866 while passenger services started on 1st March 1867. *Graham Hoare*

Helston had been the market town and focal point of the Lizard peninsula for many years, so it was natural that efforts were made to connect it with the rapidly expanding railway system. The first scheme for a railway in the area was made in 1830 in conjunction with the then flourishing mining industry, but this fell through and subsequent proposals to link Helston with Redruth, and later Camborne, also went the same way. On 9th July 1880, however, Parliament approved the Helston Railway Company's scheme for a 8¾ miles-long branch from Gwinear Road (west of Camborne) and work started on 22nd March 1882. The standard gauge line opened on 9th May 1887 to the accompaniment of great rejoicing in Helston; the line passed to the GWR in 1898. An extension to the Lizard was planned but on 17th August 1903 the GWR introduced a bus service which proved most successful and obviated the need for considerable expenditure on the extension. This was the first railway-operated motor omnibus service in the country. In addition to this claim to fame, Helston station was also the most southerly station on the network. Road competition eventually caused the branch's downfall, closure occurring from 5th November 1962. There was no Sunday service so the last trains actually ran on 3rd November. In this picture 4500 Class 2-6-2T No.4563 awaits departure from Gwinear Road with the Helston branch train on a dull 4th September 1960. *Graham Hoare*

The first station along the branch for southbound trains was Praze which served the delightfully named village of Praze-an-Beeble. This single platform station had a vitreous enamel running-in board unlike others on the line which had standard GWR-style chocolate and cream signs. The track on the right was originally a loop and was converted to a siding in about 1950: it was obviously still in use when this picture was taken on 2nd September 1961. The wooden structure at the end of the main station building was the ground frame: it was clearly well protected from the elements. *Graham Hoare*

The 2.10pm Gwinear Road to Helston train, hauled by 4500 Class 2-6-2T No.4570, pauses at the intermediate station of Nancegollan on 15th October 1960. The passing loop seen here was originally about half-a-mile north of the station but was moved to the much more operationally convenient location seen here in 1937. A new signal box, located at the north end of the up platform, was commissioned on 19th September 1937. In 1944 four sidings were laid for military use but latterly they were used to handle rapidly expanding broccoli and potato traffic. A camping coach was parked at Nancegollan from 1958 until closure. *John Langford*

The next station down the line was Truthall Halt (sometimes known as Truthall Platform) which was opened by the GWR on 3rd July 1905, when a rail motor service was introduced on the line. There was little habitation nearby so it is unlikely that the halt attracted much traffic. The line between Truthall and Helston was extremely sinuous so it would almost have been quicker for passengers to walk, bearing in mind that Helston station was poorly situated in relation to the town centre. In this picture No.4563 is seen running in with a Gwinear Road-bound working on 2nd September 1961. *Graham Hoare*

Goods trains do not come much smaller than this! A Helston to Gwinear Road train, apparently consisting of one van and a goods brake, approaches Truthall Halt in September 1961 with 4575 Class 2-6-2T No.5515 in charge. The emptiness of the surrounding countryside is evident in this illustration. Cober viaduct, the most impressive civil engineering work on the line, was situated south of Truthall Halt. Built of local granite, it was 100 yards long and 90ft above the valley floor and was sometimes referred to locally as Lowertown viaduct after a nearby village. In order to minimise engineering work the line made a horseshoe turn between Truthall and Helston. *Graham Hoare*

Rather peculiarly, if a train leaving Helston station went straight ahead it would have finished up in the engine shed, but at least the layout permitted a locomotive stabled in the shed to run straight onto its train. The 'main line' curves sharply to the right. In this view of the Gwinear Road end of the station the twenty-one lever frame signal box is prominent with the small granite-built engine shed also clearly visible. The shed was well used because the locomotive booked to power the first up train was stabled overnight at Helston. This picture is thought to have been taken in the late 1950s. *The late J.H.Moss / Stuart Ackley collection*

A further view of Helston, this time taken from the 'country' end of the station on a bright and sunny 2nd September 1961. In this quintessential branch line scene one of the footplate crew strides down the platform as a smart lady wearing a white hat and carrying a matching handbag apparently waits to board the train. Attractive flowers, on the extreme left, add further colour to the scene. Most unusually for a small branch line terminus, the station had a small privately operated refreshment room. In this picture the station seems to be alive with activity so it seems particularly sad that the line was closed forever fourteen months later. *Graham Hoare*

HELSTON BRANCH

A train to Gwinear Road, with 4500 Class 2-6-2T No.4563 in charge, awaits departure from Helston in September 1960. The station consisted of a single platform and had the appearance of a through station due to the fact that the line continued for about 200 yards along an embankment to the site of a carriage shed which was dismantled in about 1958. The goods yard, which is partially visible on the left of the shot, had a crane capable of lifting six tons. The summer 1961 timetable advertised eight Monday to Friday trains in each direction with a couple of extra services on Saturdays. The timetable also provided information about connecting Western National bus services to and from The Lizard. *Graham Hoare*

A gleaming 'County' Class 4-6-0, No.1028 *County of Warwick,* pauses at St Erth with the up 'Cornishman' in September 1960. Note the train is made up of coaches in both WR chocolate and cream and maroon liveries. The carriages on the right of the picture, presumably being employed on the St Ives branch, also add to the variety of colours – what a selection! The history of the name 'Cornishman' can be traced back to the 1890s when it was carried unofficially by a Paddington to Plymouth train but the use of the title had lapsed by around 1904. It was revived in 1935, being used on a Paddington to Penzance express for a while, but the name disappeared from the timetables once again upon the start of the Second World War. It was, however, revived for a second time in 1952, but applied to the 9.15am Wolverhampton to Penzance service and corresponding return train. In the summer 1960 timetable on Mondays to Fridays the train left Wolverhampton at 9.00am and was booked to arrive in Penzance at 5.50pm. In the reverse direction departure was at 10.30am with an arrival in the West Midlands town at 7.25pm. It was routed via Stratford-upon-Avon and ran fast between Bristol and Plymouth in both directions. *Colour-Rail*

Bodicote Grange again! No.6870 is seen once more working the 2.20pm Truro to Penzance train on 11th June 1961, but this time framed by the footbridge at the western end of St Erth station. This locomotive, one of a class of eighty, was built at Swindon in March 1939 and lasted in traffic until September 1965. *Michael Allen*

ST ERTH STATION

The counties of Devon and Cornwall abounded with really delightful branch lines but none could match the outstanding line from St Erth to St Ives. This enchanting branch is only 4¼ miles long but it manages to include a wide river estuary, dramatic scenery as it twists and turns on a ledge cut into the cliffs, and unforgettable views of golden sands and the almost Mediterranean blue sea stretching far into the distance. The view from the train window for holiday-makers starting their fortnight's break by the seaside is absolutely captivating, to say the least. No wonder the late Chris Gammell, the well-known author and photographer and connoisseur of British branch lines, said it was unquestionably his favourite line. The branch was opened on 1st June 1877 and was the last to be built to the broad gauge. In this picture, 4500 Class 2-6-2T No.4566 enters St Erth with an unidentified train from St Ives on 4th September 1960. *Graham Hoare*

The first station on the branch was Lelant and in this shot the wooden station building is reflected in the still waters of the river Hayle, which has a broad estuary at this point, on 12th August 1961. There was apparently a staff of two people at this tiny station until 1930 and one thereafter until all staff were withdrawn on 29th September 1958. Goods traffic finished in about 1956. There was a rail-served quay at Lelant in more prosperous times, the remains of which are still extant, but the rails have long since been removed. *Roy Patterson*

Another picture taken at Lelant on 12th August 1961, showing 4500 Class 2-6-2T No.4563 making a brisk getaway with the 7.25am St Ives to St Erth train. The cool, clear morning air has obviously helped to produce a splendid trail of billowing steam from the locomotive as it heads for the main line junction a mile distant. In May 1978 a new station, Lelant Saltings, was opened between St Erth and Lelant. The new premises were built adjoining a huge new car park, the idea being that people would use the train to alleviate chronic traffic congestion in St Ives. *Roy Patterson*

A train bound for St Ives rounds a tight curve between Lelant and Carbis Bay on 3rd June 1961. Motive power is provided by 4500 Class 2-6-2T No.4564: locomotives of this class were ideally suited to the line and monopolised services for many years. *John Beckett*

The only intermediate station of any note on the branch is Carbis Bay which is depicted in this photograph taken in June 1959. The premises consisted of a single platform and a waiting shelter, the stone-built station building being located at the top of the path. *Gerald Daniels*

The beach at Carbis Bay is practically deserted as 4500 Class 2-6-2T No.4566 heaves its train up the 1 in 60 climb, and around an extremely tight curve, after leaving Carbis Bay station on a grey and overcast day in September 1960. The St Ives branch is well known for its severe curvature as it twists and turns around the headlands, a feature that is exemplified in this shot. *Graham Hoare*

There was a tiny engine shed at St Ives, with an adjacent 10,000 gallon water tank, which is seen in this portrait dating from 3rd September 1960. The shed was built in 1877 and was officially a sub-shed of Penzance: it was closed in September 1961. The signal box can just be discerned in the distance on the right: it survived until 8th September 1963. Victorian villas dominate the rest of the picture as an unidentified 4500 Class 2-6-2T makes what was probably a rousing departure as the crew try to gain some momentum up the steep 1 in 60 climb towards St Erth. *Graham Hoare*

Holiday-makers flocked to St Ives in droves in the hope of experiencing endless, unbroken sunshine and lazy days spent relaxing on the beach. Alas, it did not always work out like that and 10th August 1960, when this shot was taken, appears to have been overcast with at least some rain. What a let down just at the height of the holiday season! 4500 Class 2-6-2T No.4563 poses in the station while another engine, apparently of the same class, simmers in the background. *Roy Denison*

Unsightly oil drums and an old dustbin detract from the otherwise neat and tidy station premises at St Ives. In this shot, taken on 11th June 1961, 4500 Class 2-6-2T No.4566, in quite clean condition, is seen awaiting departure with the 4.35pm passenger working to St Erth. At the time of this picture No.4566 was allocated to Penzance shed. The Great Western Railway did a great deal to promote the holiday trade at St Ives, purchasing the nearby Tregenna castle in 1878 and subsequently converting it into a hotel. *Michael Allen*

A quartet of locomotives pose at Long Rock shed, Penzance. The engines seem to have been specially positioned for photography and perhaps this was done with the help and co-operation of the shed staff. Certainly it is an attractive scene even if it is a trifle artificial. For the record the locomotives are Nos. 6824 *Ashley Grange*, 4920 *Dumbleton Hall*, 6828 *Trellech Grange*, and 6988 *Swithland Hall*. Long Rock shed dated from 1914 when it superseded an earlier shed located close to Penzance station. This shot was taken on 24th September 1960. *R.C. Riley*

Great Western steam personified! 'Castle' Class 4-6-0 No. 5069 *Isambard KIngdom Brunel*, which has been scoured to perfection, awaits departure from Penzance station with the famous 'Cornish Riviera Express' on a sunny day in June 1957. Note the small alloy headboard. This locomotive was outshopped from Swindon works in June 1938 and remained in traffic until February 1962. *Colour-Rail*